SECOND THOUGHTS ON THE DEAD SEA SCROLLS

SECOND THOUGHTS
ON THE
DEAD SEA SCROLLS

by

F. F. BRUCE, M.A., D.D.

*Rylands Professor of Biblical Criticism and Exegesis in the
University of Manchester*

Wm. B. Eerdmans Publishing Company
Grand Rapids, Michigan

First Published . . . 1956
Second Edition © The Paternoster Press, 1961

*This first American paperback edition
is published by arrangement with
The Paternoster Press, London
1964*

Fourth printing, August 1972

ISBN 0-8028-1026-8

PHOTOLITHOPRINTED BY GRAND RAPIDS BOOK MANUFACTURERS, INC.
GRAND RAPIDS, MICHIGAN

TO MY STUDENTS

IN THE UNIVERSITY OF SHEFFIELD

(1947–1959)

WHO TAUGHT ME

NEARLY AS MUCH

AS I TAUGHT THEM

CONTENTS

PREFACE

SOME years ago I wrote a little book entitled *The Dawn of Christianity* (subsequently incorporated in a larger work entitled *The Spreading Flame*). I cannot find in it any reference to the Dead Sea Scrolls. News of the Scrolls was slowly being released at the time when that book was being written, but at that time it did not seem likely that the new knowledge would make much of a contribution to the study of Christian origins. Today the situation is quite different. In the eyes of many, the new discoveries have brought about a revolution in our understanding of Christian origins. Those who have appeared slow to admit this revolution have been reproved for their unseemly conservatism, which has been put down to religious inhibition. "It is difficult," says one writer, "for the clergyman scholar to face certain implications of the contents of the Dead Sea manuscripts." He himself, we are to assume, is eager only to follow truth wherever it may lead. But so, we may be sure, is the "clergyman scholar" whom he criticizes.

Whether the following pages are the work of a scholar is for others to judge. But it cannot be urged against them that they are the work of a clergyman. A lay teacher in a secular university will perhaps be allowed some freedom from those inhibitions which are alleged to beset his ordained colleagues—but one never knows. Yet this may be said at the outset. If *The Dawn of Christianity* were being written now, and not in 1950, it would no doubt be a much better book (for it would benefit by the added experience and, we hope, wisdom of the intervening years), and it would certainly contain copious references to the Dead Sea Scrolls. But the second thoughts induced by the Scrolls would affect only incidental features of the story. The main point of view would be defended all the more confidently and vigorously because of these new discoveries.

The title of this book, then, is not *Second Thoughts on the Dawn of Christianity* but *Second Thoughts on the Dead Sea Scrolls*. For as more and more information comes to hand about these documents, earlier estimates of their significance have to be revised. Indeed, the word "second" in the title must be interpreted in a liberal sense. Some of the thoughts which find expression here are probably third, fourth or even fifth thoughts. But they are certainly not last thoughts.

Yet the outlines of the situation out of which these documents emerged are becoming increasingly clear; and unless some quite incalculable factor is suddenly introduced into the picture, it seems likely that further information, as it continues to be published, will modify a number of points here and there but in general will help to fill the outlines in and make them clearer rather than necessitate a radical reinterpretation.

I have tried to maintain a clear distinction between the new evidence itself and the inferences which I think should be drawn from it. I hope I have succeeded in this.

My grateful acknowledgments are due to Mr. David J. Ellis, who has provided the frontispiece and illustration for the dust wrapper, to Mr. David F. Payne, for the description of Masada quoted on pp. 53 f., and to my wife, for her help at every stage of the work.

September, 1956   F. F. BRUCE

PREFACE TO THE SECOND EDITION

I have taken the opportunity afforded by this revision to expand the treatment of certain points in the light of more recent knowledge, and to amend various defects in the first edition. While I have changed my mind on a number of details, my judgment on the central issues remains unchanged, and therefore this new edition can properly appear under the same title as its predecessor, *Second Thoughts on the Dead Sea Scrolls*.

September, 1961   F. F. B.

PREFACE TO THE PAPERBACK EDITION

Further reflection on the identity of the Wicked Priest, discussed on pages 100-106, has now disposed me to think that the case for Jonathan, brother of Judas Maccabaeus, is stronger than that for Alexander Jannaeus. Apart from that, the past three years have brought about no serious modifications in the main positions maintained in this book.

June, 1964

PROLOGUE

WHEN the Persian king Cyrus brought the Babylonian Empire to an end in 539 B.C., he authorized a body of Jewish displaced persons to return to their home in Judæa, from which they had been deported by Nebuchadrezzar two generations previously, and to rebuild their national shrine in Jerusalem. After some years the temple was rebuilt, and its services were carried out anew by the members of the old priestly families, at whose head stood Jeshua, a scion of the house of Zadok, which had occupied the chief priesthood in the former temple since its dedication by King Solomon about 960 B.C. down to its destruction by the Babylonians in 587. But, while the ancient chief-priestly family was restored to its sacred office, the royal house of David, which also returned from exile, was not restored to the kingship.

The new Jewish community was organized as a temple-state, consisting of Jerusalem and a few miles around. At the head of the state was the high priest, who controlled internal Jewish affairs; the wider interests of the Persian Empire were the responsibility of the civil governor of Judæa, who was appointed by the crown. When, after two hundred years, the Persian Empire was in its turn brought to an end by Alexander the Great, no material change took place in the Jewish constitution. They had a Macedonian governor over them instead of one appointed by the Persian king; they had to pay taxes to a Macedonian court instead of to the Persian court; they were exposed to the powerful influence of Hellenistic culture. But the high priests of the house of Zadok remained as before at the head of the Jewish temple-state. So matters continued under the domination of the Ptolemies, who inherited Alexander's empire in Egypt, and retained Palestine under their control until 198 B.C. When in that year they lost Palestine to the rival dynasty of the Seleucids who had succeeded to Alexander's heritage in the greater part of Asia, the transition was smooth so far as Judæa was concerned. The increasing tendency to follow western ways did indeed cause grave concern to the more conservatively-minded Jews, but they had no complaint against the Gentile government, which guaranteed the temple constitution and granted the utmost liberty in the practice of the Jewish religion.

For a variety of reasons a change came about with the accession of Antiochus IV (Epiphanes) to the Seleucid throne in 175 B.C.

Early in his reign he interfered with the Zadokite succession to the high priesthood; later he tried to prohibit the Jewish religion altogether. This led to a national and religious rising, as a result of which Judæa ultimately secured complete political independence. The leaders of this rising, the priestly family of the Hasmoneans, became the ruling dynasty in the independent state, and assumed the high priesthood in addition to the chief civil and military power. From 142 to 63 B.C. the Jews preserved their hardly won independence under the Hasmoneans, but in the latter year they lost it to the Romans, who reorganized all the territory west of the Euphrates as part of their empire. But the Romans left a Hasmonean high priest in charge of the internal affairs of Judæa for over twenty years. In 40 B.C., however, the political situation in western Asia caused them to nominate one Herod as king of the Jews, and Herod ruled Palestine from 37 to 4 B.C. in the interests of Rome. His son Archelaus, who succeeded him in Judæa, was deposed by the Roman Emperor in A.D. 6, and for the next sixty years Judæa was governed by procurators appointed by the Emperor, except for three years (A.D. 41–44) when a grandson of Herod, Agrippa I, reigned over Judæa as king. From the beginning of Herod's reign the high priests, who were henceforth appointed by Herod and his descendants, or else by Roman governors, counted for less and less, although by virtue of their office they continued to preside over the Sanhedrin, the supreme court of the Jewish nation.

Misrule by Roman procurators, combined with an increasing intolerance of Gentile control on the part of Jewish nationalists, led to the Jewish revolt of A.D. 66 and the destruction of the city and temple of Jerusalem by the Roman forces in A.D. 70. With the fall of the temple, the last vestiges of the temple constitution, together with the high-priestly office, came to an end. Judæa was placed under firmer military control than before. But in A.D. 132 a new revolt broke out, and the independence of Judæa was proclaimed under a messianic claimant who is commonly known as Bar-Kokhba. After three years of guerrilla fighting this rising was crushed. Jerusalem was rebuilt by the Romans as a completely Gentile city, and a new chapter opened in the history of the Holy Land.

This sketch of Israel's political fortunes under the Persians, Greeks and Romans may provide a framework within which we may get our bearings more easily when we consider the situation which produced the Dead Sea Scrolls.

CHAPTER I

THE FIRST DISCOVERIES

WHAT ARE THE DEAD SEA SCROLLS?

THEY are manuscripts which have come to light from time to time since the spring of 1947 in a number of areas lying northwest of the Dead Sea. But while we concentrate our attention on these recent discoveries—exciting and important as they are—it is worth remembering that other finds of a similar nature have been made in the same region at much earlier times. We shall have occasion to say something about these earlier discoveries later on,[1] but the discoveries of our own day began by accident when a goatherd of the Bedouin tribe of Ta'amireh, Muhammad adh-Dhib ("Muhammad the Wolf") by name, was grazing a herd of goats in the neighbourhood of the Dead Sea, and in a cave near the Wadi Qumran came upon a long-forgotten storehouse of Hebrew and Aramaic documents. Accounts of his adventure differ in detail, but this is how it was described in *The Times* of August 9, 1949, by Mr. G. Lankester Harding, at that time Director of Antiquities in the Hashemite Kingdom of Jordan:

> One of the goats strayed in search for better pastures, and the goatherd, looking for it up the steep rock hillside, chanced upon a small circular opening in a rock face. With pardonable curiosity he looked in cautiously, but could make out only a large dark cavern; so he picked up a stone and threw it in—and heard something crack and break. Nervously apprehensive at the unexpected result of his effort he withdrew, and returned later with a friend. Each made brave by the presence of the other, they wriggled through the small aperture into the cavern, and in the dim light could distinguish some large jars standing on the floor, one of them broken by the recently thrown stone. Fragments of others were lying all around, but they quickly proceeded to examine the contents of the intact jars.
>
> Instead, however, of the expected golden treasure they drew forth a number of leather rolls covered in, to them, an unknown writing—had they but known it, a treasure far greater than any gold.

It has commonly been supposed that the discovery was made in the spring of 1947. But the *Journal of Near Eastern Studies* for October 1957 contained a variant account, given by Muhammad

[1] See pp. 122 ff.

himself in Arabic to Mr. N. S. Khoury of Bethlehem, who wrote it down from Muhammad's dictation. According to this account, it was in 1945 that Muhammad entered the cave (unaccompanied on his first visit to it) and found the jars. He broke nine with his staff, to find that they contained nothing but some reddish seeds; but when he broke the tenth (which was sealed with a substance like red clay), he found an inscribed roll of leather inside. This he took away with him in hope that it might prove useful for sandal-straps; in fact, he gave two companions each a piece of it for that purpose. When he reached home, he put the scroll into a bag which hung there for two years. Then an uncle of his took it to Bethlehem to show to a dealer in antiquities in case it might be of any value. No doubt by the time it attained this form Muhammad's narrative had undergone something of the stream-lining process which form-critics assure us oral tradition tends to undergo as time goes on; even so, it suggests that the precise details of the discovery may be impossible of recovery. But to think of that scroll[1] hanging up in a Bedouin home for two years! We should at least be glad that the material was not really suitable for sandal-straps.

To Bethlehem at any rate the scrolls were taken in the early summer of 1947, and handed over to a general dealer in that town, a member of the orthodox Syrian community.[2] Since he was unable to make anything of the writing on them, he took them along to the Syrian Orthodox Monastery of St. Mark, in the Old City of Jerusalem. The Syrian Archbishop of Jerusalem, Athanasius Yeshue Samuel, recognized that the writing was Hebrew, but neither he nor his colleagues were able to determine the nature and significance of the documents. The Archbishop there-fore consulted several scholars in Jerusalem who might be ex-pected to advise him. Late in July, 1947, a few weeks after his monastery had bought the manuscripts, he consulted a member of the École Biblique, a splendid institution for Biblical and arch-aeological study in Jerusalem manned by French Dominicans. At this time an eminent Dutch scholar, Professor J. van der Ploeg, of Nijmegen University, was giving a course of lectures in the École Biblique, and he was taken to see the manuscripts at the Syrian monastery. He identified one of them as a copy of the Book of Isaiah in Hebrew, apparently of astonishingly early date, but when he reported what he had seen to his friends at the École Biblique, one scholar of outstanding authority in this field of study told him that it was preposterous to suppose that Hebrew

[1] Presumably the scroll of Isaiah mentioned on p. 16.

[2] An excellent account of the transaction and its aftermath is given by J. M. Allegro in *The Dead Sea Scrolls* (Pelican Books, 1956), pp. 17 ff.

manuscripts of such antiquity could exist, and that the scrolls he had seen must be fakes. Accordingly Professor van der Ploeg thought no more of the matter for the time being. (Before long, the scholars of the *École Biblique* found reason to change their minds, and no institution has exerted itself more nobly in the acquisition and study of the Dead Sea manuscripts. But at the time their scepticism was both natural and wise.)

The Syrians then approached members of the Jewish community in Jerusalem; after all, Jews might be expected to have a special interest in ancient Hebrew documents. Two librarians from the Hebrew University visited the monastery, but did not feel themselves capable of passing an opinion on what they saw, and suggested that an expert in palaeography from the University should be given an opportunity of examining the scrolls.

Towards the end of November, the late Professor Eleazar L. Sukenik, of the Chair of Palestinian Archaeology in the Hebrew University, who had recently returned from America, heard about some other scrolls from the cave at Qumran.[1] He was taken by an Armenian friend to see an Arab dealer in antiquities in Bethlehem—a different dealer from the one already mentioned— and bought from him for the Hebrew University most of the remainder of the manuscripts which had originally been taken from the cave, together with two jars in which some of the manuscripts were said to have been found. At this time he did not know of the companion manuscripts which the Syrian monastery had acquired, and when at last he heard of them, it was almost impossible for him to see them. These were the closing months of the British mandatory régime in Palestine, when tension between the Jews and Arabs was mounting rapidly, and there could be no coming and going between the Jewish and Arab areas of Jerusalem and its neighbourhood. Meanwhile Sukenik was examining the documents which he had acquired. He thought they must have come from some ancient *genizah*—a storeplace in which Jews deposited sacred writings which had become too dilapidated for ordinary use, until they could be reverently disposed of. And the more he examined them, the more his excitement increased. Two days after he made his first purchase, he wrote in his diary: "I read a little more in the 'parchments.' I'm afraid of going too far in thinking about them. It may be that this is one of the greatest finds ever made in Palestine, a find we never so much as hoped for." Shortly before Christmas he was able to buy another piece of manuscript, in very poor condition. The President of the Hebrew University, Dr. Judah L. Magnes, readily saw to it that funds were

---

[1] Professor Sukenik's account is reproduced by Y. Yadin in *The Message of the Scrolls* (1957), pp. 21–29.

made available for the purchase of the scrolls, and another colleague, Professor James Biberkraut, undertook the delicate task of unfolding them, all crumpled, decomposing and brittle as they were.

At last, about the end of January, 1948, a meeting was arranged between Sukenik and a member of the Syrian community in the Y.M.C.A. building of Jerusalem, which was situated in one of the security zones established by the mandatory government. Sukenik was shown some of the scrolls from the monastery and allowed to borrow them for a few days. From one of them, a manuscript of the Book of Isaiah, he copied several chapters for his own interest. On February 6 he returned the scrolls, and arrangements were made for another meeting, at which it was hoped the Syrian Archbishop and the President of the University would both be present, to arrange for the purchase of the scrolls by the University. But this meeting never took place.

The British mandatory government in Palestine came to an end on May 15, 1948, and in the trouble that ensued Jerusalem was divided between the two sides—the Jews and the Arabs. The Syrian monastery was in the Arab zone, and when once the fighting broke out there could be no easy communication between that zone and the Jewish zone. When, some months later, the Constituent Assembly of the State of Israel met, each member found on his desk a copy of Isa. 40 as transcribed by Sukenik from the Syrian scroll, together with an account of the scroll and notes on the text, comparing it with the traditional text. Certainly no more propitious words could have been found for the occasion than the prophet's message of consolation: "Comfort ye, comfort ye my people, saith your God."

But we are going ahead too quickly. On Wednesday afternoon, February 18, 1948, Mr. John C. Trever, Acting Director of the American School of Oriental Research in Jerusalem, was called to the telephone to hear something about ancient Hebrew manuscripts. Somewhat sceptically, he went to find that the speaker at the other end was a priest of the Syrian monastery, Father Butros Sowmy. Father Sowmy told him that "while working in the library of the Convent, cataloguing the books, he had come upon five scrolls in ancient Hebrew about which their catalogue contained no information." Remembering an earlier pleasant contact with members of the American School, he thought that they might be able to give some help in this matter.

Accordingly next day Father Sowmy and his brother, a civil servant, called at the American School with a suitcase containing five scrolls (or parts of scrolls) wrapped in newspaper, and a smaller fragment of manuscript. As cameras were not available at the moment, Mr. Trever copied some lines of the largest scroll by hand. While he was doing so, his visitors told him that the documents had really come, not from the monastery library, but from a cave near the north end of the Dead Sea, where they had been found by Bedouin.

Mr. Trever soon came to the conclusion that the Hebrew script of the scrolls was more archaic than anything of the kind he had ever seen. When his visitors left, he examined the words which he had transcribed, and was not long in recognizing part of the Hebrew text of the Book of Isaiah. Next day he visited the monastery (obtaining access to the Old City of Jerusalem through the Jaffa Gate with some difficulty), and persuaded Archbishop Samuel to allow the scrolls to be photographed at the American School. They were brought to the school for this purpose on February 21, and a beginning was made with the work of photographing them. One of the scrolls, however, was badly damaged and proved so difficult to unroll that it was decided to wait until it could be taken to some place where it could be unrolled without causing further damage. From some of the writing that was visible, it appeared that this scroll was written, not in Hebrew, but in a sister-language, Aramaic.

As soon as possible, the plates were developed and a few prints from the Isaiah scroll were sent by air-mail to Professor W. F. Albright, of Johns Hopkins University, Baltimore—perhaps the most eminent figure among living Biblical archaeologists. Professor Albright sent an air-letter by return post, in which he said:

> My heartiest congratulations on the greatest manuscript discovery of modern times! There is no doubt in my mind that the script is more archaic than that of the Nash Papyrus. . . . I should prefer a date around 100 B.C. . . . What an absolutely incredible find! And there can happily not be the slightest doubt in the world about the genuineness of the manuscript.

Professor Albright's excitement may be readily understood when we remember that at that time no Biblical manuscripts in Hebrew were known to survive much, if at all, earlier in date than the ninth century A.D. Therefore, if he was right in dating this manuscript of Isaiah around 100 B.C., it meant that the interval separating the time at which the books of the Old Testament were originally written from the time at which the oldest extant Hebrew copies were made was suddenly reduced by about a thousand years. The Nash Papyrus, which he mentioned in his letter, is a Hebrew fragment in Cambridge University Library containing the Ten Commandments, followed by the words: "The statutes and the

B

judgments which Moses commanded the [children of Israel] in the wilderness when they came out of the land of Egypt: 'Hear, O Israel, the LORD our God is one LORD, and thou shalt [love the LORD] thy God with all thy heart . . .'" This papyrus had been variously dated from the second century A.D. back to the first century B.C. (Professor Albright himself preferring the earlier dating); but in any case, if the newly discovered manuscript was older than the Nash Papyrus, the implications of the find were revolutionary. Professor Albright's confidence that the genuineness of the manuscript was beyond doubt was to be fully confirmed, but we may wonder how he could be so sure at that early stage in events, when he had only photographs to go by.

On the last day of February the Director of the American School, Dr. Millar Burrows, returned from Iraq, where he had been for two weeks. His interest was immediately captivated by the new discoveries, and he used one of the documents as the subject-matter for the remaining part of a course in epigraphy which he was conducting at the school. He told Archbishop Samuel what his judgment was on the antiquity of the scrolls, saying that the Isaiah scroll was, in his belief, the oldest known manuscript of any book of the Bible. The Archbishop was deeply impressed by this information—how deeply may be judged by the fact that within a week he had sent the scrolls to a place of safety outside Palestine. To export antiquities from Palestine without a permit from the Department of Antiquities was illegal, although the imminent break-down of an effective central authority in the land might be pleaded in extenuation.

Early in 1949 Archbishop Samuel arrived in the United States with his precious documents. He allowed them to be photographed and made an agreement permitting the American Schools of Oriental Research to publish them within a limit of three years. It should be explained here that the American Schools of Oriental Research are two in number—one in Jerusalem and one at Baghdad—and that the American headquarters of the Schools are at New Haven, Connecticut. Dr. Burrows' period of office as Director of the Jerusalem School came to an end in the spring of 1948, and he was now back in Yale University, fulfilling the duties of the Winkley Chair of Biblical Theology. He and his colleagues, Dr. Trever and Dr. W. H. Brownlee, now gave themselves to the task of preparing the scrolls for publication. As originally acquired by the Syrian monastery, the scrolls were five in number, but it soon appeared that there were in reality only four, as what had seemed to be two turned out to be severed halves of one original scroll (the scroll commonly referred to as the *Manual of Discipline* or the *Rule of the Community*).

Three of the scrolls were published in facsimile and transcription with admirable promptitude.[1] The fourth, however, which could not be unrolled for photographing in Jerusalem, continued to resist attempts to unroll it. Preparations were well advanced, however, for treating the material in a manner that would enable it to be unrolled without irreparable damage, when the stipulated period of three years expired. Despite pleas to let the American Schools retain the fourth scroll a little longer, the Archbishop insisted on taking all four of them back.

Now that the world of learning had sufficient information about the nature of the scrolls, it was hoped that some institution would be prepared to buy them. But—partly, no doubt, because of uncertainty about their legal ownership—universities and libraries were reluctant to make an offer for them. They were actually advertised for sale in the "Miscellaneous" columns of the *Wall Street Journal* in June, 1954. At length, on February 13, 1955, it was announced that they had been bought for the State of Israel, the price paid being two hundred and fifty thousand dollars. The money is being used for religious and educational work in connexion with the Syrian Orthodox Church.

Thus, nearly eight years after the discovery, the two lots of scrolls were reunited under the same owners. The Premier of Israel announced that a special museum would be built to house the newly acquired manuscripts, together with those purchased previously for the Hebrew University, and that it would be known as the Shrine of the Book.

WHAT WERE THESE DOCUMENTS?

Let us take the four acquired by the Syrian Monastery first. One of them, as has already been said, was a copy of the Book of Isaiah in Hebrew. Another was a copy of the first two chapters of the Book of Habakkuk in Hebrew, accompanied by something like a verse-by-verse commentary, also in Hebrew. The third— the one which had been torn in two—proved to be the text of a code of rules or "manual of discipline" of some Jewish religious community. We shall call it the *Rule of the Community*. The fourth was early seen to be written in Aramaic, and not in Hebrew like the other three. It was not unrolled until after its purchase by the State of Israel. The delicate task of separating the layers, which had become practically glued together, was accomplished by Professor Biberkraut. Then it became evident that in addition

[1] *The Dead Sea Scrolls of St. Mark's Monastery*, edited by Millar Burrows. Volume I: *The Isaiah Manuscript and the Habakkuk Commentary* (1950). Volume II, Fascicle 2: *Plates and Transcription of the Manual of Discipline* (1951).

to extensive decomposition of the material further damage had been caused by some corrosive ingredient in the ink; the decipherment of the writing was thus rendered peculiarly difficult. Quite soon after the scrolls were brought to America by Archbishop Samuel, Dr. John Trever had suggested that this one was probably a copy of the *Book of Lamech*, an apocryphal work mentioned in one or two ancient lists. His reason for thinking this was that a detached fragment of the scroll contained a sentence in which Lamech, the father of Noah, speaks in the first person and mentions his wife Bit'enosh.[1] But when news was released of the unrolling and deciphering of this fourth scroll in February, 1956, it was announced that it was not the *Book of Lamech*, but an expanded Aramaic paraphrase of Chapters 5 to 15 of the Book of Genesis, in which not only Lamech, but other leading figures in the narrative of Genesis (*e.g.* Abraham), tell their part of the story in the first person.[2]

The scrolls bought by Professor Sukenik in November and December, 1947, turned out to be three in number,[3] although one of them was in four pieces. This was a collection of *Hymns of Thanksgiving*, most of which open with the words: "I give thee thanks, O Lord, because . . ." Another was a most interesting work which Sukenik named *The War of the Children of Light with the Children of Darkness*. (We shall refer to it by its own shorter title, the *Rule of War*.) He loved to tell how, as he pored over this description of ancient warfare in the dark days of 1948, when shells were flying over Jerusalem, he had difficulty at times in distinguishing between the contemporary reality and the remote situation pictured in the scroll he was studying. The third scroll which he acquired was another copy of Isaiah, of which the text from Chapter 41 onwards was reasonably complete, while that of the earlier chapters had survived only in about a dozen fragments. All three of these documents were in Hebrew.

More will be said about each of them later on. But we have already seen why such importance was attached to them right from the time when their discovery was announced. If the date first assigned to them by men like Professors Albright, Burrows, and Sukenik could be established as correct, it meant that manuscripts of the Hebrew Scriptures had come to light which were

---

[1] Bit'enosh is also given as the name of Lamech's wife in *The Book of Jubilees*, another expanded paraphrase of Genesis, composed in the second century B.C. See pp. 25, 56 f., 98.

[2] A full account of this scroll, with reproduction and translation of five of its twenty-two surviving columns, is given in *A Genesis Apocryphon*, edited by N. Avigad and Y. Yadin (1956).

[3] His edition of them was published posthumously in Jerusalem: *The Dead Sea Scrolls of the Hebrew University* (1955).

older by at least a thousand years than any hitherto known. Such a claim of antiquity was naturally received with considerable scepticism. The possibility of any such discovery had been generally discounted. Old Testament textual scholars had, for the most part, resigned themselves to the indefinite acceptance of the millennial gap dividing the date of the oldest surviving copies of Hebrew Scripture from the date at which the latest parts of Hebrew Scripture were originally composed. (And the oldest parts of Hebrew Scripture were originally composed another millennium earlier still.) No less an authority than Sir Frederic Kenyon had written in *Our Bible and the Ancient Manuscripts*: "There is, indeed, no probability that we shall ever find manuscripts of the Hebrew text going back to a period before the formation of the text which we know as Massoretic"[1]—and in his last edition of the book, published in 1939, that statement was allowed to remain (p. 48), for it represented the consensus of informed opinion then as much as it had done when the first edition appeared in 1895.[2] Yet, less than ten years after the publication of the last edition, the situation was completely changed; and Kenyon himself, before his death on August 23, 1952, accepted and welcomed the reading of the new discoveries which carried the textual evidence for Hebrew Scripture a thousand years further back. Even before the new evidence came to light, Kenyon believed the Massoretic text of the Old Testament to be a trustworthy representation of what the authors had written; he lived long enough to see his belief confirmed by testimony of a kind which had hardly been thought possible.

But it was thought by several scholars that those who had so promptly assigned this early dating to the manuscripts were too hasty. Sceptical voices were raised, and it was right and proper that scepticism should be expressed. Memories were revived of famous hoaxes; some recalled, for example, the case of a Jerusalem antiquarian named Shapira, who in the eighteen-eighties had professed to discover an ancient copy of the Book of Deuteronomy, dated about 900 B.C., which he tried to sell to the British Museum for a million pounds! Shapira's claim impressed a number of

---

[1] This is the text produced by the Massoretes, editors of the Hebrew text in the schools of Palestine and Babylonia in the eighth and ninth centuries A.D., who recorded the traditional pronunciation, punctuation and interpretation of the Old Testament writings. We do, however, have evidence of another kind for the text of the Old Testament in the pre-Massoretic period; for example, manuscripts of the Septuagint (the pre-Christian Greek translation of the Old Testament) have survived which antedate the earliest extant copies of the Massoretic text by six centuries and more. I have given some account of this subject in *The Books and the Parchments*, ch. ix.

[2] In a posthumous revision of this work (1958), account is taken of the new situation created by the Dead Sea discoveries.

people, until it was subjected to remorseless scrutiny by a distinguished French archaeologist, Charles Simon Clermont-Ganneau, who proved that Shapira had written the copy himself on wide margins cut from synagogue scrolls, imitating the script of the then recently discovered Moabite Stone! In another field of study it was remembered how in the nineteen-twenties an Italian's claim to have discovered the lost writings of the Roman historian Livy succeeded for a time in deceiving an eminent English Latinist.

Such claims demand the most sceptical examination. If they are false, the sooner they are exposed the better. If they are valid, their validity will be all the more securely established if they have stood the severest tests. There is a genuine scepticism which St. Paul has recommended to us in the words: "Test everything; hold fast what is good" (I Thess. 5: 21). And this genuine scepticism which tests everything is an ally to true faith, not an enemy.

In America a distinguished Jewish scholar, Dr. Solomon Zeitlin of Philadelphia, has over the years ventilated almost every argument that could conceivably be urged against the antiquity of the scrolls in the *Jewish Quarterly Review*, of which he is editor.[1] (It must be immediately added that he has, with admirable impartiality, extended the hospitality of its pages to defenders of the scrolls' antiquity.) No English scholar has gone to such lengths as Dr. Zeitlin. But when the first announcements of the discovery were made, Professor Godfrey R. Driver of Oxford played a salutary part in exposing the weaknesses of some arguments adduced in support of the antiquity of the scrolls, and in demanding the most incontrovertible evidence for claims which he thought were being too lightly advanced.[2] Questions like the character of the ruling and the composition of the ink should be investigated, he urged, to test the conclusions which the palaeographers had announced. He did not *deny* the earlier dating, but he thought that those who adhered to it should bear other possibilities in mind. More recently he has advocated a date in the period following A.D. 70, on the ground that the scrolls contain references to persons and incidents of the war with Rome.[3]

---

[1] He summed up his criticisms in a monograph, *The Dead Sea Scrolls and Modern Scholarship* (1956), but has added to them in subsequent numbers of the *Jewish Quarterly Review*.

[2] See, *e.g.*, his lecture to the Friends of Dr. Williams's Library, *The Hebrew Scrolls* (1950).

[3] *E.g.* in a lecture to the Royal Central Asian Society, "The Dead Sea Scrolls: The Riddle Unriddled", reported in the *Daily Telegraph*, June 20, 1957. A similar view is defended by C. Roth in *The Historical Background of the Dead Sea Scrolls* (1958).

CHAPTER II

LATER DISCOVERIES

The First Cave

IT was plainly of great importance that the cave where the manuscripts were said to have been found should be visited as soon as possible by an impartial commission of investigators, competent to assess the various lines of evidence. Dr. Burrows tells[1] how he and his colleagues at the American School tried to arrange a visit in March, 1948, but the arrangements fell through. Soon after that, fighting broke out between the Arab states and Israel, and a visit was out of the question so long as hostilities lasted. When at last a truce was called to the fighting, and the frontier between the opposing sides was patrolled by United Nations observers, the northern half of the western shore of the Dead Sea lay within the territory of the newly extended Hashemite Kingdom of Jordan. Thanks to the help of a Belgian officer among the United Nations observers, Captain Philippe Lippens, who was personally interested in the discovery of the scrolls, it was possible for a party to visit and inspect the cave in February, 1949. Mr. G. Lankester Harding, the Director of Antiquities for Jordan, took charge of the excavation of the cave, with the co-operation of Father Roland de Vaux, of the Dominican *École Biblique.*

It was immediately evident that they had been forestalled by other investigators, who found their way to the cave in November or December, 1948, cut a more convenient opening into it, lower than that through which the Bedouin goatherd had first entered, dug up the floor of the cave and threw some of the débris out through the new entrance. This inexpert excavation destroyed much of the evidence which the official party might otherwise have found and interpreted. One of the unofficial investigators left a clue to his identity behind in the shape of a cigarette-roller bearing his name; Mr. Harding was able later on to give it back to him and tell him where he had left it. It was probably as a result of the illegal excavation that the Syrian monastery acquired three fragments of the Book of Daniel from two separate scrolls; one of these fragments contains the passage in Dan. 2:4 where the Hebrew text of the book gives way to Aramaic.

[1] In his book, *The Dead Sea Scrolls* (1955), p. 16.

The expert excavation of the cave was carried on with the utmost care; in consequence, several hundred fragments of inscribed leather or parchment and a few papyrus fragments were discovered. Most of these fragments were so small and brittle that the excavation had to be done with penknives, tweezers, small brushes and fingers; otherwise irreparable damage would have been done. No intact jars were found, but there was an abundance of broken sherds, and also several pieces of the linen in which the scrolls had been wrapped before being put into the jars.

The use of jars to keep scrolls in was natural and widespread in antiquity. There are early Egyptian examples of this practice, and the Old Testament records how the prophet Jeremiah, on the eve of the Babylonian exile, deposited the purchase-deeds of a field near Jerusalem in an earthenware vessel, so that they might be preserved safely until the people returned from captivity (Jer. 32: 14). A first-century Jewish work entitled the *Assumption of Moses* tells how Moses handed his writings to Joshua with instructions to steep them in cedar oil and place them in earthenware jars. (The cedar oil was calculated to preserve the skin or leather on which the words were written; it is possible that some of the Qumran scrolls were treated in this way before being wrapped in linen.)

The fragments recovered from the cave included portions of other Biblical books in Hebrew—Genesis, Exodus, Leviticus, Deuteronomy, Judges, Samuel, Isaiah, Ezekiel, and the Psalms. Seven fragments of Isaiah proved to belong to the imperfect scroll of that book which the Hebrew University secured in November, 1947. The fragments of Leviticus were written in an archaic script—the "Phoenician" or Palaeo-Hebrew character in which Hebrew was written in earlier days, before the "square" letters which we now associate with Hebrew came into use for the writing of that language. Previously the square letters were used in writing Aramaic, but towards the end of the third century B.C. they came to be used for writing Hebrew too, displacing the older Phoenician characters. Does this mean that the Leviticus fragments belong to a manuscript written at a time when the Phoenician script was in common use for writing Hebrew? Some have thought so; one scholar would date it as far back as 450 B.C. But in the case of this manuscript we are possibly dealing with a standardized professional literary script which continued to be used for two or three centuries without much change. Even so, these Leviticus fragments have claims to be regarded as older than any of the other documents found in the cave.

There were also fragments of non-Biblical works—commentaries on Micah, Zephaniah and the Psalms; apocryphal works like the

Book of Jubilees, the *Book of Noah*, and the *Testament of Levi*; works dealing with the life and worship of a religious community; collections of hymns, and so forth.

As the news of these discoveries spread, the excitement of scholars increased, and a bewildering variety of views were ventilated on the date, origin, meaning and purpose of the scrolls. The actual discovery and publication of the documents reflected a high degree of co-operation between Muslims, Jews and Christians of varying traditions at a time when racial and religious animosities were burning fiercely in Palestine and the surrounding territories. Professor Sukenik, for example, made public acknowledgment of his gratitude to Christians and Muslims of Bethlehem for the aid which he, a Jewish scholar, received from them in securing the scrolls which he purchased for the Hebrew University in the later part of 1947. Unfortunately, a similar degree of friendly co-operation (or at least mutual tolerance) was not always evident on the part of some scholars who engaged in what has been called "The Battle of the Scrolls." However, the dust of that battle has largely cleared away. As more and more discoveries have been made, and their results published, the main outlines at least of the answers to questions about the date and provenance of the manuscripts have become increasingly discernible.

OTHER CAVES

For some time it was taken for granted that the cave in which all these discoveries were made was the only cave of its kind in the area. But the local Bedouin were more optimistic. The original finders of the manuscripts had not realized the importance which the world of scholarship would attach to their discoveries. But now their fellow-tribesmen in their simplicity argued that if manuscripts were found in one cave, there might be further manuscripts awaiting discovery in other caves with which the sides of the Wadi Qumran and neighbouring water-courses were honeycombed. So they began to explore the area thoroughly, and in a few caves their diligence was rewarded. News got around that further scrolls were available for purchase, and the prices now being charged by the finders were considerably stiffer than those which Muhammad adh-Dhib and his comrades had received for the original lot. To be sure, this private enterprise was illegal, for antiquities ought to be handed over to the government authorities. But in the case of such fragile antiquities as these, the finders must be treated diplomatically, lest the precious documents should be sold to dealers or tourists and dispersed, or otherwise lost or destroyed through careless handling or exposure to damp. Learned institutions throughout the world were invited to co-operate in the acquisition of the manuscripts. Where the archaeological authorities of Jordan got on the track of fresh discoveries, they enlisted the goodwill and co-operative help of the Bedouin who had forestalled them. A fixed payment of £1 for each square centimetre of inscribed material was agreed with the finders, and by such means further caves were explored and more finds were made. Thus far eleven caves in all in the Wadi Qumran have yielded treasure of this kind. These caves are conveniently designated by numbers. The cave where the original discoveries were made is naturally known as Cave 1—more concisely, 1Q, where Q stands for Qumran—and the others are numbered Cave 2, Cave 3, and so on. Caves 3, 5, 7, 8, 9 and 10 were discovered by archaeologists, the others by Bedouin.

THE COPPER SCROLL

In Cave 3 a unique discovery was made—inscribed rolls not of skin or papyrus but of copper. There were two rolls, but one of them consisted of two strips of copper rolled up together. It looked as if they were originally riveted end to end to form a sheet of metal about eight feet long by one foot high. It was plain from the outside that they contained writing, but what the writing had to say was not easy to determine. The rolls could not be unrolled because the copper was completely oxidized. At last, at the end of 1955 and the beginning of 1956, they yielded to expert treatment in the Manchester College of Technology, under the direction of Professor H. Wright Baker of the Chair of Mechanical Engineering. A spindle was put through the rolls; the rolls were coated with glue, baked hard in an oven, and cut into strips with a tiny circular saw. Each strip was photographed as it was cut, and dust and débris were removed from the remaining part, stage by stage, by vacuum suction and a dental brush.

The text thus revealed consisted of about 3,000 letters, and so carefully and skilfully had the operation been carried out that not more than five per cent of the text was destroyed, and of the rest only about two per cent was illegible. The lettering bore signs of having been hastily punched out (with about ten punching blows to a letter), and the scrolls were rolled up hurriedly by unskilled hands. The language is what is known as colloquial Mishnaic (post-Biblical) Hebrew; this is the earliest known text in this kind of Hebrew.

Simultaneous announcements of the contents of these scrolls were made on May 31, 1956, in Manchester and Amman. They contained an inventory of sixty-one hoards of treasure—gold, silver, incense and the like. This treasure, according to the inscription, had been deposited in a number of hiding-places, some in the region of Jericho and the north-west shore of the Dead Sea, but most in the vicinity of Jerusalem. The exact localities indicated would be difficult to identify at this time of day; three samples of the directions were quoted in the first announcement, as follows:

> . . . In the cistern which is below the rampart, on the east side, in a place hollowed out of rock: six hundred bars of silver . . .
> . . . Close by, below the southern corner of the portico at Zadok's tomb,[1] and underneath the pilaster in the exedras, a vessel of incense in pine wood and a vessel of incense in cassia wood . . .
> . . . In the pit near by towards the north, near the graves, in a hole opening to the north, there is a copy of this book, with explanations, measurements and all details . . .

All the material for the perfect treasure-hunt, especially if the second copy of the inventory is located! Some of the hoards were evidently buried 16 to 18 feet underground; the total weight of the gold and silver, on a literal interpretation, would amount to nearly 200 tons, but in this and certain other respects we have probably to reckon with a code of some kind.[2] When, for example, we are told of two water pitchers which between them held 80 talents of gold, we should have to envisage each of them as capable of containing 15 hundredweight, unless "talent" could be taken as a code-word for something much smaller, perhaps "mina" (one-sixtieth of a talent).

The most probable interpretation of this document is that it lists various items of treasure from the Jerusalem temple which were stored here and there during the struggle of A.D. 66–70, possibly to serve as sinews of war as occasion might require. Why this copy of the inventory should have been hidden in one of the Qumran caves is uncertain. There is no need to connect it directly with the Qumran community; it is more natural to link it with some of the Zealots or other Jewish war-leaders of the time.

The opening and reading of the copper scrolls disposed of the widely held theory that they contained a set of rules and regulations nailed to the wall of the community headquarters. But it must also be pointed out that the announcement in some degree confirmed the view earlier expressed by Professor K. G. Kuhn of Heidelberg University, who in 1953 examined as much of the

[1] Possibly one of the tombs in the Kidron valley, east of Jerusalem; but we have no clue to the identity of this Zadok.

[2] Some of the locations also appear to be indicated in code; thus the Mount Gerizim where one of the hoards is said to be hidden is probably a place near Jericho and not the well-known mountain of that name near Shechem.

writing as was decipherable in reverse on the outside of the copper scrolls, and concluded that they contained a record of the community's treasures and the places where they were hidden when the headquarters were abandoned.[1]

Fuller information about the contents has been provided more recently. In the July 1959 issue of the *Revue Biblique* Abbé J. T. Milik supplied a French translation of the whole document, with notes on the places mentioned. Then in 1960 Mr. J. M. Allegro had a book published, entitled *The Treasure of the Copper Scroll*, in which for the first time the complete Hebrew text was reproduced, together with an English translation, an account of the discovery and decipherment of the document, and detailed discussion of many of the place-names and other terms occuring in the text.

Thousands of Fragments

Some 40,000 manuscript fragments have been recovered from the Qumran caves. The cave which yielded the greatest abundance of literary treasure was Cave 4. Tens of thousands of manuscript fragments were recovered from this cave. These fragments had once constituted about 380 separate books. About 100 of these books were part of the Bible. Every Old Testament book except Esther is represented among them; some Old Testament books are represented several times over. In addition to Hebrew and Aramaic scriptures, the Greek version is also represented. Some Septuagint fragments of two manuscripts of Leviticus and one of Numbers have been identified from Cave 4; Cave 7 has yielded fragments of the Septuagint text of Exodus and also of the *Letter of Jeremiah*, which appears in most editions of the Apocrypha as the last chapter of Baruch, although it is an independent composition. From all the Qumran caves about 500 separate books have been identified, a few of them being almost intact, but the great majority surviving only in fragments.

The latest cave so far to yield manuscript treasure is Cave 11, which was discovered by Bedouin early in 1956, a little way north of Cave 1. From Cave 11 were acquired several remarkably well preserved portions of scrolls—remarkably well preserved, that is to say, when one considers that they were not stored in jars, as the manuscripts in Cave 1 were. (The significance of the fact that the Cave 1 scrolls were stored in jars, while those in the other Qumran caves were not, has not yet been satisfactorily cleared up.) Among these most recent acquisitions are a beautiful small scroll

---

[1] *Cf.* his article, "Les Rouleaux de Cuivre de Qumran," in *Revue Biblique* 61 (1954), pp. 193 ff.

of part of Leviticus in palaeo-Hebrew script, a fine tightly-rolled Psalter (unfortunately lacking its lower quarter), the core of an Ezekiel scroll, several large fragments of an *Apocalypse of the New Jerusalem*, and an Aramaic paraphrase or "targum" of the book of Job.[1] Up to the time of writing a number of other manuscripts from this cave appear to be still in Bedouin hands.

In addition to books of the Bible, then, the discoveries from the caves include apocryphal works, such as the Hebrew and Aramaic fragments of the *Book of Tobit* discovered in Cave 5; uncanonical works, such as the *Book of Jubilees*, the *Book of Enoch*, the *Testament of Levi*, and so forth; several works hitherto unknown, such as the *Apocalypse of the New Jerusalem* (known from three or four other caves as well as Cave 11); commentaries and paraphrases, collections of hymns, and documents with a bearing on the beliefs and practices of some religious community. It was a reasonable working hypothesis that this might have been the community to which the books originally belonged, and that some at least of the rest of the literature discovered might provide a clue to the special interest of that community. The *Rule of the Community* found in Cave 1, and represented also by ten fragments found in Cave 4, appeared to offer specially full information about the ideals and organization of the community. It was not long before affinities were detected between it and another ancient Jewish work which was discovered some fifty years before. This work, extant in two fragmentary manuscripts written between the tenth and the twelfth centuries A.D., was found in the genizah of the synagogue in Old Cairo, along with many other documents of comparable date. It falls into two parts—an *Admonition* and a selection of *Laws*—and was produced early in the first century B.C. within a Jewish community which cherished the priestly traditions of the sons of Zadok. For this reason it is frequently described as the *Zadokite Work*,[2] and the community in which it was produced has been called the community of the Zadokites, or (from other references in the fragments) the New Covenanters. It was therefore specially significant that further

---

[1] This document is described as the earliest written targum hitherto known. That it should be a targum of Job is the more interesting because we have independent testimony from the Babylonian Talmud (tractate *Shabbath*, 115a) to the existence of a written targum of this book in the first century A.D., which the great Gamaliel ordered to be built into the temple walls (presumably not later than A.D. 63, the year in which the reconstruction begun by Herod was finally completed). The Septuagint version of Job has an additional note at the end, which is said to be "translated from the Syriac book" (presumably from an Aramaic targum). Opinions differ on whether the *Genesis Apocryphon* from Cave 1 should be regarded as a targum; much depends on the precise definition of "targum".

[2] It is also frequently called the *Damascus Document*, from its references to a period of exile in the land of Damascus. See p. 121.

fragments of the *Zadokite Work* turned up in the Qumran caves 4, 5 and 6, which have enabled us to supplement the text already known to us. There is now no doubt that the community referred to in the *Zadokite Work* was identical with that described in the *Rule of the Community*, although the two treatises may not reflect the same stage in the history of the community.

All these fragments from the caves have had to be subjected to a lengthy and delicate process of cleaning, unfolding, smoothing out, and placing between glass. Infra-red photography brings to light writing which the naked eye can no longer discern. The task of piecing together the fragments which originally belonged to one and the same book is not an easy one. It is least difficult where the book is already well known (a book of the Bible, for example); but where the book in question has been completely unknown hitherto, the task is not an enviable one. It is worse than trying to reconstruct a jigsaw puzzle when most of the pieces have disappeared and pieces from other jigsaws have become mixed up with the pieces that remain.

Until June 1960 an international team of scholars was engaged on this tedious but fascinating work in the Palestine Archaeological Museum, in a long room set apart for this purpose, familiarly known as the "Scrollery." A full report of all the fragments recovered from Cave 1 (apart from the seven major documents found in 1947) was published in the first volume of a series entitled *Discoveries in the Judaean Desert*, edited by Fathers D. Barthélemy and J. T. Milik (Clarendon Press, Oxford, 1955). Other volumes (ten or more) are to follow as soon as the various bodies of material are ready for publication. Volume II contains the material from the Wadi Murabba'at, south of Qumran, about which we shall have something to say in our next chapter; Volume III contains the material from the remaining Qumran caves apart from Caves 4 and 11. The material from Cave 4 will occupy five or six double volumes.

CHAPTER III

WADI MURABBA'AT AND KHIRBET MIRD

WADI MURABBA'AT

ABOUT the same time as it became known that manuscripts had been found in other caves at Qumran over and above Cave 1, news began to circulate about other manuscript discoveries made in the Wadi Murabba'at, which runs down to the Dead Sea from the west about eleven miles south of the Wadi Qumran and some fifteen miles south-east of Jerusalem. Early in 1952 Bedouin of the same tribe as had discovered the first manuscripts at Qumran were found to be offering for sale pieces of leather with Hebrew and Greek writing on them. The archaeological authorities of Jordan learned that these fragments had come from the Wadi Murabba'at, and when they arrived on the spot with eight Bedouin whom they had brought along to do any necessary digging, they found thirty-four other Bedouin hard at work on their amateur excavations. A number of these were immediately taken into service to carry on the good work under lawful and expert supervision. Four caves in the area contained traces of human occupation at six distinct periods in antiquity—in the Chalcolithic Age (fourth millennium B.C.), the Middle Bronze Age (c. 2000–1550 B.C.), the Iron Age (more specifically the eighth and seventh centuries B.C.), the Hellenistic period, the Roman period and the Arab period.

From the third, fourth, fifth and sixth of these periods written documents were discovered. From the third period, the era of the later kings of Judah, came a papyrus palimpsest inscribed in Phoenician (palaeo-Hebrew) characters. The earlier writing seems to have been a letter; superimposed on it is a list of four names with symbols and numbers. From the fourth period come two inscribed potsherds belonging to the late second century B.C. From the sixth period came some paper documents in Arabic. (To this period, too, we must assign some woollen textile from one of the caves, for which the radio-carbon test[1] indicated an early seventh-century date.) But it was from the fifth period, the Roman era, that the most interesting material came.

In A.D. 132, when Hadrian was Roman Emperor, a revolt broke out in Judæa against the Romans. The leader of this revolt was

[1] See p. 45.

a man named Simeon, who struck coins designating himself as
"Simeon Prince of Israel" and bearing such significant dates as
"Year I of the Redemption of Israel"; "Year II of the Liberation
of Israel." But his leadership was not purely secular in character; some people believed him to be the long-expected Messiah
who would lead Israel to victory against her heathen oppressors.
Among those who recognized Simeon as the Messiah was the
greatest religious teacher of the day, Rabbi Aqiba. Aqiba hailed
Simeon as the conquering hero foretold long ages before by the
Mesopotamian prophet Balaam. "A star," said Balaam, "shall
come forth out of Jacob"; and he went on to describe how this
"star" would crush the enemies of Israel, while Israel under his
leadership would perform valiant deeds and exercise dominion
(Num. 24: 17–19). Because Aqiba identified Simeon with this
predicted "star," Simeon came to be known as Simeon Bar-
Kokhba, which is Aramaic for "Simeon son of the Star." There
were others who would not acknowledge Simeon's claims (including the Jewish Christians, who naturally could not recognize
anyone other than Jesus as the true Messiah); they preferred to
call him Simeon Bar-Koziba, which means "Simeon the son of
falsehood." Simeon maintained a fierce guerrilla resistance
against the Roman forces for over three years, and exacted a
heavy toll from them before his revolt was crushed in A.D.
135.

Some of the documents from the Roman era of occupation in
the Wadi Murabba'at made it quite clear that Simeon's followers
maintained a garrison here, under the command of one Yeshua
Ben-Galgolah. Two letters written to Yeshua by Simeon were
found, which incidentally showed that Bar-Kokhba and Bar-
Koziba were both plays on the wording of Simeon's proper
patronymic, which was Ben-Kosebah.[1] That is what he calls
himself in these letters. Here is the text of one of them:

> From Simeon Ben-Kosebah to Yeshua Ben-Galgolah and to the
> men of your company. Peace! I call heaven to witness against
> me that if one of the Galilaeans whom you have protected troubles
> us, I will put fetters on your feet as I did to Ben-Aflul. Simeon
> Ben-Kosebah, Prince of Israel.

Who the luckless Ben-Aflul was, or what he had done, we cannot
tell. Nor do we know anything about the Galilaeans mentioned
in the letter. There is no particular reason to think that they were
Jewish Christians. We know that Jewish Christians had to endure
considerable persecution at the hands of Simeon and his sup-

---

[1] *Ben* is Hebrew for "son"; *bar* is the corresponding Aramaic word.

porters, because they refused to join his rising, but there is no evidence that they were called Galilaeans. It is safest to suppose that the letter refers to certain troublesome individuals from Galilee of whom no further information is available to us.

There was also a letter addressed to Yeshua by two officials of a Jewish community. A well-preserved deed of sale in Aramaic —called the Kephar Bebhayu conveyance—is dated "in the third year of the liberation of Israel" (A.D. 134).[1] Among other dated documents from the second century are some Greek texts on papyrus—a marriage contract dated A.D. 124 (in the seventh year of Hadrian), a contract of reconciliation between a husband and wife, a bond from the year 171, and a document dated in the reign of the Emperor Commodus (A.D. 180–193). There were also some fragments in cursive Latin. This suggests that when the revolt was suppressed, the post was occupied by a Roman garrison for a considerable period.

A few inscribed potsherds (ostraca) were found, most of which bore Hebrew writing, though the writing on some was Greek. Two fragments of Greek literary works were deciphered: one of these was religious in character, the other seemed to deal with the family of Herod, as the names Salome and Mariamne could be distinguished. Could it be a fragment of the work of Nicolas of Damascus, historiographer-royal at the court of Herod the Great? The fragment is too small to lead to any certain conclusion.

But the second-century discoveries on this site included many fragments of Biblical Hebrew manuscripts, written on leather. Among these were fragments of four scrolls—one of Genesis, two of Exodus and one of Deuteronomy—which bore unmistakable signs of having been violently torn up. Was this destruction the work of the Roman soldiers when they stormed the position? It would not have been the first time that Roman soldiery had treated Jewish scripture in this way. Other manuscripts had been reduced to fragments by humbler members of God's creation than Roman soldiers; rats and other small animals had used them to make nests. There was the beginning of a scroll of Isaiah, still showing verses 4 to 14 of Chapter 1. There was a complete phylactery—that is to say, a parchment containing four passages from the Hebrew Bible (Ex. 13: 1–10; Ex. 13: 11–16; Deut. 6: 4–9; Deut. 11: 13–21) in parallel columns, which was placed in a leather container and worn on the forehead or the left arm in literal fulfilment of the divine injunction: "And these words which I command you this day . . . you shall bind them as a sign upon your hand, and they shall be as frontlets between your eyes"

---

[1] The earliest dated document of the Roman period found at Murabba'at is an Aramaic contract from the second year of Nero (A.D. 55–56).

C

(Deut. 6: 6, 8). (Fragmentary phylacteries were found in some of the Qumran caves, but these were of an older type, which included the ten commandments in addition to the passages mentioned above; this type went out of use after A.D. 70.)

From unidentified caves in the neighbourhood of Murabba'at the Bedouin produced another group of manuscripts (mostly fragmentary) very similar in character to those found in the Wadi Murabba'at. Some of them appear to have originated with another insurgent garrison of A.D. 132–135, for they included a Hebrew letter addressed to Simeon Ben-Kosebah and two Aramaic contracts dated "in the third year of the liberation of Israel by the hand of Simeon Ben-Kosebah." There were also two Greek documents and two Aramaic documents dated by the era of the Roman province of Arabia (which was founded by the Emperor Trajan in A.D. 106), and papyrus documents in the Nabataean dialect of Aramaic, longer than any Nabataean documents previously known. Biblical Hebrew texts from this unidentified cache included fragments of Genesis, Numbers, and the Psalms, together with another complete phylactery; there was also a fragmentary copy of a Greek version of the Minor Prophets, showing a text in agreement with that used by Justin Martyr in the middle of the second century A.D.; it has been hailed as an important missing link in the history of the Septuagint. More recently there has come from Murabba'at a scroll of the Minor Prophets in Hebrew, from Joel 2: 20 to Zechariah 1: 4, belonging to the second century A.D. and closely related to the Massoretic text.

These discoveries have no direct connexion with those made in the Qumran caves. But they do have an important indirect bearing on the Qumran manuscripts. Many of the documents from Murabba'at and the unknown site in the same area are definitely dated in the second century A.D. The Biblical texts found along with them will not be later in date than these. It follows, in that case, that the Qumran manuscripts are earlier than the second century A.D., and that for two reasons. In the first place, the Murabba'at documents show a later stage in the evolution of Hebrew and Aramaic handwriting than the Qumran documents do. In the second place, the Biblical Hebrew texts at Murabba'at conform exactly to the consonantal text preserved by the later Massoretes; they reflect an age when textual deviations such as appear in several of the Biblical texts from Qumran had been removed from currency—largely, no doubt, through the activity of Rabbi Aqiba and his colleagues about the beginning of the second century. The Murabba'at texts, then, afford external confirmation of the general dating already established on other grounds for the Qumran manuscripts.

DISCOVERIES IN ISRAEL

Farther south along the west shore of the Dead Sea one crosses from Jordan into Israel. Early in 1960 further discoveries from the period of the Ben-Kosebah revolt were made in caves in this area, but on the Israeli side of the frontier. These caves, like those at Murabba'at, were evidently used as guerrilla outposts during the revolt. Among the documents found there were two scroll fragments inscribed with Exodus 13: 1–16, and a small fragment containing parts of seven lines of Psalm 15. In one of the caves eleven arrow-heads and shafts were discovered; other discoveries include a coin of the revolt and a palm-leaf basket holding a unique set of nineteen Roman pieces of brass, possibly legionary cult vessels, including twelve libation jars, three incense shovels, a pan, two large bowls and a large key. On the handle of one of the jars was a figure of the Egyptian god Serapis; this was badly scratched. It has been thought that the whole collection of vessels was captured by the insurgents in a sortie, and the likeness of the pagan deity dutifully defaced. In a goatskin bag a papyrus package, folded fifteen times, was found, together with various articles of feminine property, such as weaving material, skeins of wool, a spinning wheel and a mirror. From a vulture's nest in the vicinity a sock was recovered, with the name of a member of the neighbouring communal settlement of En-gedi sewn on. Professor Yadin remarked that, but for this mark of identification, someone would probably have tried to date the sock, such are the preservative qualities of the dry atmosphere there. (See pp. 155 f.)

KHIRBET MIRD

Midway between the Wadi Qumran and the Wadi Murabba'at yet another watercourse runs down to the Dead Sea from the west—the Wadi en-Nar, better known to Bible readers as "the brook Kidron" which lies between Jerusalem and the Mount of Olives. To the north of this watercourse, about nine miles southeast of Jerusalem, lie the ruins of a Christian monastery of the Byzantine period, now called Khirbet Mird (on the site of the earlier fortress of Hyrcanion). Here in July 1952, the indefatigable Ta'amireh unearthed further manuscript material of great interest, but of considerably later date than the documents found at Qumran and Murabba'at. These included papyrus fragments of private letters in Arabic from the seventh and eighth centuries, a Syriac letter (also on papyrus) written by a Christian monk, and a fragment of the *Andromache* of Euripides in Greek, together with a number of Biblical texts in Greek and Palestinian Syriac. The Greek texts included fragments of uncial codices of Wisdom, Mark, John and Acts, written between the fifth and eighth centuries A.D.; those in Palestinian Syriac included fragments of Joshua, Luke, John, Acts and Colossians (many of these were palimpsests). All these Biblical fragments were of Christian origin, unlike those from Qumran and Murabba'at, which belonged to Jews.[1]

---

[1] *Cf.* G. R. H. Wright, "The Archaeological Remains at El Mird in the Wilderness of Judaea", with an appendix by J. T. Milik, *Biblica* 42 (1961), pp. 1 ff.

CHAPTER IV

DATING THE FINDS

FROM the earliest announcement of the discoveries there has been much disputation about the date of the manuscripts. It is not a bad thing that this has been so. It would be a thousand pities, when the issues at stake are so important, if the pronouncements of even the most eminent and competent scholars were accepted without question. Fortunately, in these fields of study (as in others), scholars are rarely disposed to accept one another's dicta, especially when these dicta are so revolutionary in substance and in implication.

But in the ardour of debate there has at times been a tendency to confuse questions that should be kept distinct. When we talk about the date of the scrolls, we should realize that at least three separate questions are involved:

1. *When were the works represented by the various manuscripts originally written?*

2. *When were the manuscripts themselves copied?*

3. *When were the manuscripts deposited in the caves?*

The first and second questions coincide only when we are dealing with an autograph, the manuscript actually written by the author himself or by someone else at his dictation.[1] For example, if (by a long stretch of the imagination) we were to light one day upon the actual draft of the prophet Isaiah's earlier oracles which he sealed up and handed to his disciples for safe keeping, according to Isa. 8: 16, the date of the manuscript would be identical with the date of the original draft—734 B.C. But, in point of fact, we have no manuscript of any of Isaiah's prophecies anything like so old as that. The earliest manuscript of his prophecies that we know of is the complete scroll of the Book of Isaiah found in Cave 1 at Qumran, and if it is to be dated (as seems probable) in the second century B.C., then nearly six hundred years separate it from the original draft which Isaiah wrote or dictated. In the actual state of affairs, the answers to Questions 1 and 2 are quite distinct, so far as Biblical manuscripts are concerned.

---

[1] Like the Ben-Kosebah correspondence or legal documents found in the Murabba'at caves (pp. 32 ff.).

1. *When were the works represented by the various manuscripts originally written?*

This is a question which must be answered firstly by a careful study of the contents of each work (that is to say, by internal evidence), and secondly by considering any allusions which may be made to the work in question in other documents which can be dated independently (that is to say, by external evidence). This line of approach belongs to the discipline sometimes known as "higher criticism"—a branch of study which is by no means confined to Biblical literature.

As concerns the Biblical writings found at Qumran, we have already ample internal and external evidence for coming to conclusions about their date and authorship. The new discoveries add scarcely anything to our knowledge in this respect. But our evidence is much scantier for many of the non-Biblical works which have come to light.

A good example of the position is provided by a manuscript which combines a Biblical text with something else. The commentary on the Book of Habakkuk discovered in Cave 1 contains the Hebrew text of part of that book together with a commentary on the text. Obviously the Hebrew text of Habakkuk must be earlier in date than the commentary appended to it. The internal and external evidence for the date of the one will be quite different from the evidence for the date of the other.

The Book of Habakkuk as we have it now consists of two compositions. One of these, contained in Chapters 1 and 2, is entitled "The oracle of God which Habakkuk the prophet saw"; the other, contained in Chapter 3, is entitled "A prayer of Habakkuk the prophet, according to Shigionoth," and is actually a psalm, complete in itself. The Qumran manuscript has the text of the first two chapters only, with a running commentary, and it is plain from the state of the manuscript that it never contained the text of the third chapter. Possibly the *Oracle of Habakkuk* and the *Psalm of Habakkuk* were regarded as two distinct works.

The internal evidence of the first two chapters of Habakkuk suggests that they were composed somewhere in the land of Judah around the year 600 B.C. The author laments the oppression which he sees on every hand, and wonders why God does not intervene to defend the right against the rulers of his nation who pervert justice. He is told that a judgment is about to befall these unrighteous rulers; the Chaldeans will invade the land and sweep them from their misused eminence. Later, the prophet complains that the Chaldeans are even more oppressive than the Jewish rulers who fell before them, and he receives further assurances that God will accomplish His purpose and vindicate His righteousness in His own good time. Since we know that the Chaldeans became a power to be reckoned with in Judah and the neighbouring lands in 605 B.C., and that they occupied Jerusalem in 597 B.C. and destroyed it in 587 B.C., it is easy to conclude that the various parts of the first two chapters of Habakkuk are to be dated in the course of these years. The title of these two chapters—"The oracle of God which Habakkuk the prophet saw"—gives the prophet's name.

As regards external evidence, the earliest we have is a statement in the Septuagint, prefaced to the legend of Bel and the Dragon (one of the apocryphal additions to Daniel), which mentions Habakkuk's prophecy and describes him as "Habakkuk the son of Joshua of the tribe of Levi." The tradition that he was a Levite may be true, but the part which he plays in the story of Bel and the Dragon is as unhistorical as the rest of the story. All that this external evidence indicates, then, is that about 100 B.C. (the approximate date of the Greek version of Bel and the Dragon) Habakkuk the prophet and his prophecy were well known and were believed to belong to the period of the Babylonian exile.

Of course the internal and external evidence for the date of the prophecy of Habakkuk has no direct bearing on the Dead Sea Scrolls; it has been discussed here merely to illustrate how such evidence is recognized and used. What does directly concern us is the evidence for the running commentary attached to the text of Habakkuk's prophecy in the manuscript which we are considering.

This commentary is in itself "external" evidence for the existence of Habakkuk's prophecy at the time when the commentary was written; it also shows clearly that at that time Habakkuk's prophecy was venerated as holy writ. But how are we to decide the time at which the commentary was written? If we can determine the date at which the scrolls were deposited in Qumran Cave 1, and if, further, we can determine the date at which this particular scroll was copied out, we shall know that the composition of the commentary cannot be later than these dates. Thus far there does not seem to be any more direct external evidence that would enable us to date the composition of the commentary. But internal evidence should in any case be considered first. What does the internal evidence for the commentary amount to?

One thing is plain; the commentator believes that the prophecy which he is concerned to interpret is being fulfilled in his own day, and he describes persons and events of his own day so as to show that Habakkuk was really foretelling *them*. Unfortunately for us, he describes those contemporary persons and events in such an allusive style that scholars are not yet in agreement about their identity. Can we identify them with persons and events already known in history?

Habakkuk had spoken of the rise of the Chaldeans and their conquering advance—things which took place in his own lifetime. But the commentator does not think that Habakkuk really meant to speak of the Chaldeans and their empire; in actual fact, he maintains, Habakkuk was describing in advance imperial conquerors of the commentator's day. Habakkuk *said* the "Chaldeans" but he really *meant* the "Kitti'im"—people who, at the time when the commentator was writing, had come from across the sea, were imposing their yoke on all lands, and would soon invade the land of Israel. The question then is: Who were these "Kitti'im"—the people of "Kittim"? Originally the term Kittim denoted Cyprus (or even more particularly the Phoenician settlements around Kition, the modern Larnaka); but it came more generally to mean the Greek islands and coastlands of the Eastern Mediterranean. In the Book of Daniel it is used of the Romans (Dan. 11: 30), possibly because the incident referred to there was regarded as the fulfilment of an ancient oracle of Balaam in which ships from Kittim are mentioned (Num. 24: 24).

If an imperial conqueror from the Mediterranean lands is sought to satisfy the commentator's description of the Kitti'im, then we may think either of Alexander the Great and his successors or of the Romans. The suggestion made at one time, that they are to be identified with the Crusaders of the eleventh and twelfth centuries A.D., is really put out of court by the contents of the commentary, as well as by all that we can discover about the age of the manuscript and the time at which it was deposited along with its companions in the cave.

If we consider Alexander and his successors to be denoted by the Kitti'im, then the reference will probably be more particularly to the Seleucid king Antiochus IV (175–163 B.C.), whose attempt to suppress the ancestral religion and customs of the Jewish nation led to the patriotic rising under Judas Maccabaeus and his family, of which we may read in the Books of Maccabees.[1] But there are some reasons for thinking that the commentary reflects the conditions of the following century. A companion commentary on Nahum[2] indicates that an interval of time elapsed "from Antiochus to the rulers of the Kitti'im"; whichever Antiochus is meant,

[1] The ablest statement and defence of this identification of the Kitti'im is given by Professor H. H. Rowley in *The Zadokite Fragments and the Dead Sea Scrolls* (1952), and "The Kitti'im and the Dead Sea Scrolls", *Palestine Exploration Quarterly* 88 (1956), pp. 92 ff.

[2] See p. 78.

the expression supports the identification of the Kitti'im with the
Romans rather than with the Seleucid forces. And we shall in
due course consider other arguments for seeing the Romans in
the Kitti'im.[1] The Habakkuk commentary in that case would be
written shortly before the occupation of Judæa and Jerusalem by
the Roman general Pompey in 63 B.C.

2. *When were the manuscripts themselves copied?*

Sometimes a scribe with an accurate turn of mind will indicate
the date on which he begins or completes a manuscript; such an
indication is the best evidence we could desire for determining
when a manuscript was copied. But evidence of this kind is almost entirely wanting at Qumran. There are one or two dated
contracts, such as one from Cave 4 dated in the reign of the
Emperor Tiberius (A.D. 14–37); but the vast majority of the documents are quite undated.

There is, however, one branch of study which is particularly
helpful in determining when an undated manuscript was written.
This is the study known as palaeography—the study of ancient
handwriting. We know how in more recent times the style of
handwriting tends to vary in our own country from generation
to generation. Our grandfathers used a different style of handwriting from ours—and one, it must be added, which was much
more legible and pleasing to look at. So too in more remote
times styles of handwriting varied from one generation to another
and from one country to another. This means that the date of a
manuscript can be determined, within reasonable limits, by the
characteristics of the writing which it exhibits. Greek and Latin
palaeography has been studied for such a long time, and has such
an abundance of material to work upon, that it has become almost
an exact science. Classical palaeographers usually find themselves in general agreement about the dating of Greek and Latin
manuscripts from the closing centuries B.C. down to the invention
of printing in the fifteenth century A.D. and later still.

Hebrew and Aramaic palaeography has for long been at a dis-
advantage as compared with Greek and Latin palaeography in that
it has not had nearly so much material to work upon so far as the
pre-Christian era and the earlier centuries A.D. are concerned.
None the less it is as exact a science in principle as any other branch
of palaeography. And it is worthy of note that the scholars who
have examined the Dead Sea manuscripts on the basis of palaeography have for the most part agreed upon an early date for them—
that is to say, a date in the closing centuries B.C. or the early years

[1] See pp. 71 ff.

A.D. The scholars who have argued for a considerably later date are not palaeographers; some of them, indeed, have gone so far as to dismiss the palaeographical evidence as worthless—an odd example of obscurantism from an unwonted quarter!

It was the palaeographical evidence that from the outset convinced Sukenik and Albright of the antiquity of the scrolls, and the palaeographical evidence still supplies the main proof of their antiquity, although there is, as we shall see, further corroborative evidence of other kinds.

In fact, the palaeographical evidence can be dismissed only if it is shown that the scrolls are fabrications of a later age, deliberately written in an archaic script so as to deceive readers, and planted in order to be "discovered," like the Piltdown skull, at an opportune moment. There have been fakes of this sort in the past. But they have been detected and exposed very quickly, as soon as they were submitted to competent judges, like Clermont-Ganneau, who exposed the Shapira fraud, or Tischendorf, who exposed the Simonides forgeries.[1] But never have ancient manuscripts been viewed with greater scepticism, or subjected to more rigorous examination, than these Qumran documents. All the circumstances of their finding rule out the possibility of deliberate fraud; the Bedouin who have discovered them are not the sort of people who could manufacture the fragments which are proving such a windfall to them; and prudent administrators of museums and libraries are not likely to pay large sums of money for their acquisition without being satisfied of their value. Dr. H. J. Plenderleith, Keeper of the Research Laboratory at the British Museum, speaking of some fragments from Cave 1 which had been submitted to him for special treatment, said that "twenty-five years of experience in the handling of antiquities had convinced him at once that the materials were genuine, a conviction which was, subsequently, fully justified when the fragments were submitted to scientific examination."[2]

Among Semitic palaeographers in Great Britain, Dr. S. A. Birnbaum, of the London School of Oriental and African Studies, occupies a position second to none. He is at present publishing the material on which the science of Hebrew palaeography is based in a great work entitled *The Hebrew Scripts.* His verdict on the date of the first published scrolls was given in a valuable little study on *The Qumrân (Dead Sea) Scrolls and Palaeography* (1952); the Habakkuk scroll, he held, was copied between 100 and 50 B.C.; the *Rule of the Community* between 125 and 100 B.C.,

[1] Constantine Simonides, a hundred years ago, produced a number of fakes, including several allegedly first-century fragments of the New Testament.

[2] *Journal of Transactions of the Victoria Institute* 82 (1950), p. 146.

and the complete Isaiah scroll (Isaiah A) between 175 and 150 B.C. Later he has assigned the incomplete Isaiah scroll (Isaiah B) to a date between A.D. 1 and 25, and the *War*, *Hymns* and *Genesis Apocryphon* scrolls from Cave 1 to a somewhat later date.[1] The complete Isaiah scroll's greater antiquity than its companions is further attested by signs of wear and tear; it had clearly been used for quite a long time before it was deposited with the others in the cave.

Dr. Birnbaum's relative dating of these scrolls is generally accepted by other palaeographers, although they show a tendency to prefer rather lower absolute dates—roughly a quarter of a century lower in each case.

The abundance of manuscript material provided by the caves explored from 1952 onwards has advanced the study of Hebrew palaeography beyond all expectation. Four hundred distinct scribal hands have been distinguished at Qumran, providing an adequate basis for comparative study. A clear distinction can now be made between the development of the more formal book-hand and the less formal cursive script used for everyday purposes. The book-hand was used by preference for Biblical manuscripts; the cursive was used commonly for community documents and Aramaic works. All stages of the evolution of these two hands are represented in the Qumran caves from the third century B.C. to the first century A.D. The older Phoenician (palaeo-Hebrew) script also appears to have survived in use for certain purposes longer than was formerly realized, and to have been employed side by side with the book-hand and cursive forms of the square script.

Further evidence of a rather later stage in the evolution of the square script has been forthcoming from the manuscript finds in the Wadi Murabbaʿat and its neighbourhood. Several of these latter documents, as we have seen, bear explicit dates in the second century A.D., and thus supply a reliable criterion for fixing the chronology of other stages in the evolution.

Questions have been asked about the composition of the ink and the ruling of the scrolls with guiding lines (horizontally, to keep the lines of writing straight, and vertically, to keep the edges of the columns straight). Does a study of these things throw any light on the date of the manuscripts?

In a letter to *The Times* of September 22, 1949, Professor G. R. Driver suggested that an analysis of the ink might provide information about their date. Was it a metallic ink or not? "If it is metallic, they are likely to be later than the Mishnah (c. A.D. 200);[2]

---

[1] *Palestine Exploration Quarterly* 92 (1960), p. 25.

[2] But Dr. Birnbaum says there was iron in the ink used for the Lachish Letters in 588/7 B.C.!

but, if it is non-metallic, they may be earlier, even though in this case the test will be inconclusive, as non-metallic ink may have continued in use beside metallic ink for many centuries." The analysis, when it was carried out, was quite conclusive in a chemical sense. No metal was present in the ink; carbon alone was used. But this simply meant, as Dr. Plenderleith pointed out, "that the nature of the ink cannot be regarded as vital evidence for dating purposes".[1] It does not exclude the dating assigned to the scrolls by the palaeographers.

Nor does the ruling of the writing material give us any more positive indication. The use of guiding lines to keep the writing straight is of quite considerable antiquity. Ruled papyri have been found belonging to the first century A.D. and even earlier. And if it was found necessary to rule papyrus, the fibres of which are usually sufficiently straight and parallel to serve as natural guiding lines, how much more necessary must it have been to rule the smooth surface of a skin which was prepared to receive writing!

The composition of the ink and the nature of the ruling, it appears, neither confirm nor contradict the paleographical findings. The palaeographical findings point fairly definitely to the last two or three centuries of the Second Jewish Commonwealth (the period ending A.D. 70) as the time within which the Qumran manuscripts were copied.

3. *When were the manuscripts deposited in the caves?*

It looks very much as if the manuscripts found in the Qumran caves represent a large library which was moved from its usual headquarters because of the approach of some danger. But this likelihood does not help us very much in our endeavour to decide *when* the library was moved, because history knows of so many dangerous situations in that part of the world. "Palestine has had a long and troubled history," said Professor Driver in 1950, "and the fugitives who hid these Scrolls in the cave near Jericho might be fleeing not from the persecution which Antiochus Epiphanes set in motion (165 B.C.) nor from the invasions of the Romans (63 B.C., A.D. 70 and 135) nor even from those of the Persians (A.D. 614) or of the Arabs (A.D. 637) but perhaps merely from some local tumult caused by racial or religious hatred of which history has preserved no record."[2]

But there are certain lines of evidence which enable us to choose to some degree among these diverse possibilities. The scrolls

---

[1] *Journal of Transactions of the Victoria Institute* 82 (1950), p. 146.
[2] *The Hebrew Scrolls*, p. 50. The cave referred to is Cave 1.

deposited in Cave 1 were wrapped in linen and placed in earthenware jars. Can any conclusion be reached by an examination of
the linen and the earthenware?

First, the linen. Very recently a new method of dating organic
material from its radiocarbon content—a method known as the
"Carbon 14" method—has been devised.[1] This method, still in
its experimental stage, is used to determine how long ago an
organic substance ceased to "live." Linen is, of course, an organic
material, and the application of the Carbon 14 method to a piece
of linen would aim at showing the approximate date at which the
flax was cut. In 1950 four ounces of the linen in which the scrolls
were wrapped were tested by this new technique in the Institute
for Nuclear Studies of Chicago University. On January 9, 1951,
Professor W. F. Libby, who had conducted the test, reported
that it yielded A.D. 33, with a margin of 200 years before and
after, as the date when the organism died—i.e. when the flax from
which the linen was made ceased to grow. (A later test of the
linen, carried out at Pittsburgh, indicated a dating between
250 B.C. and A.D. 50.) Naturally, the linen would be manufactured soon after the flax was cut. The linen need not have
been quite new when the scrolls were wrapped in it, but it would
not have been extremely old. The scrolls, moreover, may have
been kept in these linen wrappings before they were deposited in
the caves. But the results of the Carbon 14 method, for what
they are worth, fit quite well into the general picture which is
gradually being built up on the basis of other kinds of evidence.

What of the jars in which the Cave 1 manuscripts were stored?
Earthenware articles intended for use and not for ornament did
not have a longer life in antiquity than they do in our day. If,
therefore, the scrolls were placed in the jars at the time when they
were deposited in the cave, we should not expect the age of the
jars to go back very much earlier than the date of the deposit. The
value of pottery for establishing chronology has been increasingly
recognized over the past seventy or eighty years, the first archaeologist to appreciate its significance properly being Sir Flinders
Petrie. Styles of pottery change with surprising suddenness at
irregular intervals, but within these intervals they tend to persist
with little variation over a remarkably wide area. And as earthenware pots are by far the commonest articles made by human
hands, layers of human occupation on ancient sites can be dated
with reasonable accuracy by a study of the immense quantities of
potsherds found in successive layers. In default of expressly

[1] A simple account of the principle involved is given by Sir Mortimer Wheeler
in his Pelican book *Archaeology from the Earth* (1956), pp. 50 ff.; cf. K. M.
Kenyon, *Archaeology in the Holy Land* (1960), p. 35.

dated inscriptions there are few criteria which can be so confidently used for archaeological dating as the pottery criterion. The jars found with the manuscripts in Cave 1 are of an unusual type; no wonder, for it appears from their shape that they were specially manufactured to contain the scrolls. They are cylindrical in form, about two feet high and ten inches in diameter, and were provided with inverted bowls to serve as lids. In some cases the decomposition of the edge of a scroll near the opening of its jar formed a pitch-like substance which effectively sealed the jar; this explains why a few scrolls, in unbroken jars, were preserved in such good condition while the majority slowly disintegrated throughout the centuries because of exposure to air and moisture and the attentions of various small animals.

But if the type of the jars could not be paralleled from ordinary domestic ware, the texture of the pottery proved to be characteristic of the early Roman period.

The remains of earthenware lamps found in Cave 1 represent types known to be characteristic in part of the late Hellenistic period and in part of the Roman period.

A more definite result, however, is provided by a jar of exactly the same type as those used to accommodate the scrolls, which was discovered on a site near the caves in association with other objects which could be dated with absolute precision. This site was the headquarters of the community to which the manuscripts belonged, and to it we must now turn our attention.

CHAPTER V

KHIRBET QUMRAN

ON a rocky shelf on the north side of the Wadi Qumran, nearly three-quarters of a mile west of the Dead Sea, lie ruins which have long been known by the name Khirbet Qumran.[1] In 1873 the French archaeologist Clermont-Ganneau, whose name has already been mentioned in connexion with the exposure of the Shapira forgery, paid some attention to these ruins, although he was more interested in an ancient cemetery which lies between them and the Dead Sea. But he came to no definite conclusion as a result of his investigations.

When the first official archaeological party visited Cave 1 in 1949, they wondered if there might be any connexion between the discoveries in the cave and the ruined site of Khirbet Qumran. A trial excavation was made on the site, but nothing was found which suggested any connexion. In November and December, 1951, however, three rooms of the ruined building were excavated. In the floor of one of these rooms a jar was found of exactly the same type as those found in Cave 1, and along with it was a coin dated A.D. 10! Obviously there was more connexion between Khirbet Qumran and the manuscript deposit than they had thought; further exploration of the site must be undertaken. Accordingly systematic campaigns of excavation were carried out in the spring of 1953, 1954, 1955 and 1956. The Jordanian Department of Antiquities, the Dominican *École Biblique* and the Palestine Archaeological Museum co-operated in this enterprise.

It soon became evident that the building formed the headquarters of a large and well-organized community. Not long after the systematic excavation of the site began, Father de Vaux expressed his belief that they had located the headquarters of the Jewish sect of the Essenes referred to by the first-century Roman writer Pliny the Elder. For Pliny said that these people lived on the west shore of the Dead Sea, above En-gedi (which actually lies some twenty miles south of Khirbet Qumran).

It is with the community which occupied the building that the cemetery which lies to the east of it is most probably to be associated. We know of no other occupation which could have given rise to so many burials of such a uniform pattern. There are about 1200 burials, laid out in parallel rows lying north and south

[1] Tentatively identified with "the City of Salt" mentioned in Joshua 15: 61.

with the head to the south (only one exception has been noted to this rule). It was thus evident that they were not Muslim burials, for Muslim burials are orientated east and west. (On the other hand, it is said that the Mandaeans of Iraq[1] bury their dead with a north-south orientation.) The Qumran burials were as simple as could be; the bodies were not accompanied by funeral offerings, nor even placed in coffins. Each was laid face upwards in a small mortuary chamber at the bottom of a trench. The entrance to the mortuary chamber was then walled up with a layer of unbaked brick or a stone slab; the trench was filled in, and the burial was marked on the surface by two upright stones with a row of pebbles between them. A few potsherds in the earth filling of the graves point to the period during which the neighbouring ruins were occupied by the community. In an eastern extension of the cemetery skeletons of four women and one child were found. This fact, together with some others of a different kind which will be mentioned in due course, may suggest that, if we are indeed dealing with the remains of an Essene community, we should think of that exceptional group of Essenes mentioned by Josephus as practising matrimony, as distinct from all the other Essenes, who were devoted to celibacy.

Two subsidiary cemeteries have also been identified, one to the north and one to the south of the Wadi Qumran. In the former the sexes appear to be mixed; in the southern one four graves were cleared, and of these two contained remains of women and the other two of children of seven or eight years old. The type of burial was the same as in the main cemetery.

Researches on the site of Khirbet Qumran show that it was occupied at various times in antiquity. At a low level the remains of walls and pottery were found which belonged to the period known to archaeologists as Iron Age II (the eighth and seventh centuries B.C.). One of the potsherds found at this level was inscribed with Phoenician characters of the kind used for writing Hebrew at that time. A royal seal stamped on a jar-handle was also found. Besides, a deep circular cistern, which was in use many centuries later, clearly belongs to this period. A reasonable suggestion is that this building, belonging to the time of the Hebrew monarchy, illustrates a statement made about King Uzziah of Judah (c. 790–740 B.C.) in II Chron. 26: 10, that "he built towers in the wilderness, and hewed out many cisterns."

At the other end of the record there is evidence of brief and sporadic occupation of the site in the Arab period.

But chief interest attaches to the abundant evidence for the

[1] See p. 136.

occupation of the site in the Graeco-Roman period. In this period the following phases of occupation can be distinguished:

Ia.   Occupation (*c.* 130 B.C.) by people who cleared the circular cistern, built two rectangular cisterns beside it, constructed a few rooms around these, and installed two pottery kilns in the Iron Age enclosure.

Ib.   Occupation of a much enlarged area, with buildings of two and three storeys, and an elaborate system of cisterns (incorporating those of the earlier phase), connected by channels and supplied by an aqueduct from a dam constructed to catch the water which runs down the Wadi Qumran during the rainy season. This phase began shortly before 100 B.C.; it was brought to an end by an extensive fire and a severe earthquake, the latter of which can be dated precisely to 31 B.C.

II.   Occupation of a restored building-complex, which followed the lines of Phase Ib fairly closely, but was reinforced at a number of points against the risk of further earthquake-damage. This phase came to an end about A.D. 68, when the place was destroyed by fire, after some fighting.

III.   Occupation by a Roman garrison between A.D. 68 and 90 or thereby.

IV.   Occupation by Jewish insurgents in the second war against Rome, A.D. 132–135.

The fact that the reconstruction of Phase II followed the lines of the Phase Ib settlement so closely suggests that the building was used for the same purpose throughout these two phases, and in all probability by a religious community. (It is a reasonable, but not a necessary, supposition that it was the same community, in an earlier and weaker stage of its existence, that settled in the area during Phase Ia.) Father de Vaux's view that the building-complex in its latest extension must be identified with the Essene headquarters mentioned by Pliny is supported by the fact that no comparable ruins are known between Jericho and En-gedi.

The main building occupied by the community as its headquarters in Phases Ib and II was roughly 120 feet square, constructed of large undressed stones, with a strong tower at the north-west corner. There were several large rooms, suitable for assembly-rooms or refectories. The largest room thus far excavated, on the south of the main building, seems to have served as the main assembly hall; adjoining it was a smaller room containing over 1,000 earthenware vessels—all the varieties

D

necessary for kitchen and dining-room use. These vessels were probably made on the premises, for the excavations have revealed the best-preserved pottery factory thus far known from ancient Palestine, complete with kilns and levigating pit. It is well within the bounds of probability that the jars which accommodated the scrolls were manufactured here too.

And not only the jars, but some of the scrolls which they contained, may well have been produced in this building. For a first-storey room in the south-west part of the building was evidently furnished as a writing-room or *scriptorium*. It contained a long bench of plaster, moulded on a brick framework, on which the writers may have sat, holding the scrolls on their knees, which were raised slightly by the use of a plaster footrest.[1] That these plaster structures were intended to be used by scribes seems to be confirmed by the discovery in the same place of two inkwells, one earthenware, and one bronze. The earthenware one had the dried remains of carbon ink still adhering to its inner surface. Two plaster hand-basins found along with them have been explained as basins where the scribes might perform the ritual washing of their hands which was called for when the name of God had to be written.

No manuscripts have been discovered in the building hitherto, apart from a practice copy of the Hebrew alphabet belonging apparently to Phase Ib.

Flour mills, storage bins, ovens, a laundry, a stable, smelting furnaces and workshops with metal implements are among the other installations laid bare on the site. Evidently the community which was centred on this place aimed at being as self-sufficient as possible.

There do not appear to be residential or sleeping quarters within the building-complex; tents or the neighbouring caves could have served the members for study and rest.

One of the most striking features of the whole area was the elaborately organized water-supply. Water was brought from the higher ground to the north-west in a carefully constructed aqueduct, about a mile and a half in length, which ran west and south of the building and emptied itself into a number of well-plastered cisterns. Several of these cisterns had stone steps leading down into them, which give them the appearance of swimming-pools or baptisteries. It has sometimes been thought that these were used for ritual purification. This was a reasonable supposition in a way, for we know that a number of baptist sects flourished in the

---

[1] The higher structure has more commonly been explained as a writing-table and the lower one as a bench; but that the interpretation given above is more probable has been shown by B. M. Metzger in "The Furniture in the Scriptorium at Qumran", *Revue de Qumran* 1 (1958–59), pp. 509 ff.

Jordan valley and neighbourhood in the years before and after the commencement of the Christian era. The Essenes practised regular ceremonial ablutions, and this practice seems to be attested in the Qumran *Rule of the Community*. Others, however, have thought it to be more likely that the community used fresh water for these ablutions, such as was available in the Jordan, a few miles to the north-east, or in the spring of Ain Feshkha, two miles to the south. In that case the elaborate water-supply would be required for the domestic and industrial requirements of a fair-sized community, reckoned to have been two or three hundred strong. Similarly constructed water reservoirs are known from other Palestinian sites. The last word has not yet been said on this question.

The largest of the cisterns, to the east of the area, had fourteen stone steps leading down into it. These steps show a central crack running all the way down from top to bottom, so that their eastern half has sunk about a foot and a half below the level of the western half. This crack was a result of the earthquake which damaged the rest of the building. When the community resumed occupation of the site several years later, this cistern could no longer be used (it could not now retain water, and the damage was too extensive to be easily repaired); it was replaced by a new cistern south-east of the building. Other major repairs had to be undertaken at the same time; the north-western tower was reinforced and the walls were generally strengthened. But the general ground-plan was preserved and the building obviously continued to serve the same purposes as before.

The earthquake which caused this damage has been identified, quite convincingly, with one which Josephus describes as having devastated Judæa in 31 B.C., the seventh year of the reign of Herod the Great, who was engaged in a war with his Arabian neighbours across the Jordan at the time.

We have said that when a beginning was made with the excavation of the site in 1951, a coin of A.D. 10 was found in close conjunction with a jar of identical type to those found in the caves. Later excavation has brought to light some 650 coins of the Graeco-Roman period, by which the successive stages of occupation can be dated with reasonable certainty. The record of the coins starts in the reigns of the Seleucid King Antiochus VII (139–129 B.C.) and the contemporary Hasmonean ruler John Hyrcanus (135–104 B.C.) and carries us forward without a break to the reign of the last Hasmonean king, Antigonus (40–37 B.C.), those from the reign of Alexander Jannaeus (103–76 B.C.) being particularly frequent. But from the long reign of Antigonus's successor, Herod the Great, only five coins have turned up to

date. The record is resumed in the reign of Herod's son Archelaus
(4 B.C.–A.D. 6), and from then we have a further continuous series
of coins taking us on to A.D. 68—from Archelaus, from the
Roman procurators of Judæa under the Emperors Augustus (A.D.
6–14) and Tiberius (A.D. 14–37), a silver coin of Tyre dated A.D.
29, a specially large number of coins of Herod Agrippa I (A.D.
37–44), and several of the procurators of Judæa under Claudius
(A.D. 44–54) and Nero (A.D. 54–66).

During the revolt of A.D. 66–70 the Jewish insurgent authorities
struck their own coins. Of these there were found in the ruins at
Qumran seventy-three belonging to the second year of the revolt
(A.D. 67), but only five belonging to the third year (A.D. 68).
Contemporary with these coins of the revolt are coins minted in
the coastal cities of Caesarea, Dora and Ashkelon, which may
reasonably be regarded as pieces from the pay of Roman soldiers.
These and later coins were found in the level of the military
barracks constructed within the ruins, evidently for the use of the
Roman garrison which was stationed there for some years. This
particular coin record comes to an end about A.D. 90. Thirteen
coins from Phase IV bear witness to the presence of an insurgent
outpost at Qumran during the Ben-Kosebah revolt of A.D. 132–135;
these include one coin of Vespasian (A.D. 69–79), three of Trajan
(A.D. 98–117), and one Jewish coin of the type struck by the
insurgent leaders during the revolt.

When we assess the chronological evidence of coins, it is worth
reminding ourselves that, while coins are not used before they are
struck, they remain in use for many years after they are struck.
Silver coins continue in use much longer than copper coins, but
the coin record at Qumran consists almost entirely of copper
coins.[1]

Phase II of the occupation of Khirbet Qumran by the community was brought to an end neither by a voluntary withdrawal
nor by an earthquake, but by the violence of fire and sword. The
destruction was much more thorough than that caused by the
earthquake nearly a hundred years before. The walls were de-
molished, a layer of black ash covered the site, and a quantity of
arrow-heads added their silent testimony to the general picture.

A sample of charcoal from the room where the large stack of
earthenware vessels was found was subjected to the radio-carbon
test. A date of A.D. 16 (with a margin of deviation of 80 years

---

[1] A hoard of five hundred and sixty-three silver coins was discovered in
1955, hidden in three pots in the floor of a room on the west of the building.
These were of two kinds: coins of Antiochus VII (139–129 B.C.) and tetra-
drachms of Tyre (the latest of which was dated 9 B.C.). But these coins were
probably hidden there between 9 and 4 B.C., while the building was still in
ruins, and had nothing to do with the community.

either way) was reached for the age of the wood, and a date of
A.D. 66 (with a similar margin of deviation) for the burning.[1]

If Josephus's account of the earthquake of 31 B.C. throws light
on the damage wrought at the end of the first period of the
building's occupation by the community, another part of his
narrative helps to account for the destruction which marked the
end of the second period. For he relates that in May of A.D. 68
Vespasian, commander-in-chief of the Roman army in Palestine,
occupied Jericho, and from there the tenth legion advanced against
Jerusalem in the following year, leaving a garrison in Jericho.
What contacts the community at Qumran may have had with the
insurgents we cannot say. They may have made common cause
with one of the insurgent groups, considering that, although this
was not exactly how they had envisaged the eschatological struggle
between the sons of light and the sons of darkness, this was mani-
festly the long-awaited struggle, from which they could not remain aloof. On the other hand, their headquarters, so well
adapted for defence purposes, may have been commandeered by
the Zealots, with or without their approval. In any case, a stronghold like theirs was bound to receive hostile attention from the
Roman forces in the district. We can scarcely doubt, then, that
it was destroyed by the Romans about this time; and there is no
further trace of any connexion between the community and its
former headquarters.

Even after the storming of Jerusalem by the Romans in September of A.D. 70, there were still a few pockets of Jewish resistance left to be mopped up. Of these the one that held out longest
was at Masada, on the west shore of the Dead Sea, about twelve
miles south of En-gedi. Masada has been excavated in recent
years by Israeli archaeologists. One young Englishman who was
taken on a sightseeing expedition around those parts by bus in
March, 1956, gives the following description:

> We parked at an army camp at the foot of Masada, and set off
> skywards. Single file was the only possibility, and at places that
> was pretty difficult. I was amazed that some quite elderly folk climbed
> with us. When we reached the top, the chief guide said a few words,
> and we looked round and rested. They are busy just now excavating
> Herod's palace. The ruins of a Byzantine church were very interest-
> ing, too; but we had all too little time to investigate. We descended
> by the N.W. route—the one by which the Romans eventually
> entered; and by the way I must in passing take off my hat to the
> Romans for even attempting to capture the fortress. The first part
> of this route was the worst, and it took the hundred and eighty of us
> two and a half hours to do it; so that the rest of the descent had

[1] F. E. Zeuner, *Palestine Exploration Quarterly* 92 (1960), pp. 27 f.

to be done by the light of one torch and half a moon! At the worst
spots soldiers lent a hand, but I was asked to assist at one nasty
precipitous bend, so behold me prancing about on a narrow ledge in
the moonlight, assuring others that there was nothing to fear. We
finally reached the bottom at 9.30 p.m., after which we swathed
ourselves in blankets or sleeping-bags, and found the softest rocks
we could.

There was thus military activity west of the Dead Sea for some
years after the destruction of the community headquarters, and
the ruined site suggested itself to the Romans as convenient headquarters for a garrison. A few rooms were therefore built over
the ruins, and occupied by a Roman garrison which kept watch
over that part of the Dead Sea coast and helped to protect the
lines of communication of their comrades who were engaged
in the arduous siege of Masada. Nor did they leave the site
when Masada was captured; they remained in occupation for
ten or twenty years. This military occupation of Khirbet Qumran
is represented, as we have seen, by a number of coins ranging in
date from the last two years of Nero's reign to A.D. 90. A coin of
Herod Agrippa II, of date A.D. 86, was found outside the building;
it is uncertain whether it should be connected with the Roman
military occupation or not.

The brief occupation of the site by an insurgent garrison during
the second Jewish revolt was followed by the complete demolition
of the surviving fortifications of Qumran.

A SUBSIDIARY SETTLEMENT

Some two miles south of Khirbet Qumran, in the date-palm[1]
oasis of 'Ain Feshkha, what appears to have been a subsidiary
settlement was discovered in 1956 and excavated early in 1958.
This settlement appears to have been an agricultural centre for the
tending of flocks and the cultivation of vegetables, fruit and even,
on a small scale, grain. It was smaller than Khirbet Qumran, but
evidently had a similar history, as the evidence of coins and
articles of earthenware indicates. It was put up towards the end
of the second century B.C., and was abandoned during the last
decades of the first century B.C., to be reoccupied from the beginning of the Christian era to the revolt of A.D. 66–70, when it
was at least partially burned. It was later occupied by insurgents
in the war of A.D. 132–135. Two openings on the east side of the
building led into an inner court surrounded by rooms serving

---

[1] There are no date-palms there now, and this can only be explained on the
assumption of their destruction by man, since in undisturbed natural conditions
'Ain Feshkha would be a thriving date-palm oasis.

various purposes. To the south was a large paved enclosure, possibly used for drying dates. North of the building was a large courtyard, half of which was occupied by a system of water-channels and reservoirs, probably used for fish-breeding.[1] This discovery helps us to understand how the community could maintain its existence in the wilderness of Judæa.

[1] F. E. Zeuner, *Palestine Exploration Quarterly* 92 (1960), pp. 33 ff.

CHAPTER VI

THE SCROLLS AND THE OLD TESTAMENT

THE CANON OF SCRIPTURE

PLAINLY the Qumran sectaries were keen students of the Hebrew Scriptures. If we may judge from the fact that certain Old Testament books figured among the discoveries much more frequently than others, they would appear to have had a special interest in Deuteronomy, Isaiah, the Psalms, the Minor Prophets, and Daniel. But where so much has been left to the chances of time and tide, we can make but tentative inferences of this kind. Similarly, we cannot be too sure what to think of the fact that no fragment of the Book of Esther has been identified thus far among the Qumran finds. We know that some Jews, like some Christians in earlier and more recent times, had doubts about the fitness of Esther to be included in the canon of sacred books; on the other hand, the absence of any fragment of Esther from Qumran may be accidental.

It is difficult to make a definite pronouncement on the limits of the biblical canon recognized by the Qumran community. It is clear that they recognized the Law and the Prophets, the first two divisions of the Hebrew Bible, as divinely inspired. The commentaries which are written on those books, or on excerpts from them, presuppose that they are to be treated as divine oracles, whose interpretation was a closely-guarded mystery until it was made known in the latter days to the Teacher of Righteousness, the revered leader of the Qumran community. The Psalter was evidently accorded the same recognition as the Law and the Prophets. But what about the other books in the third division of the Hebrew Bible—the 'Writings'? We cannot simply infer that they were regarded as canonical from the fact that all of them (except Esther) are represented in the Qumran literature, for many other books are represented in the Qumran literature. The Qumran library evidently included many apocalyptic and pseudepigraphic works which enjoyed considerable prestige in certain sections of the population of Judæa in those days, such as *Jubilees* and *First Enoch*, which appear to be closely related to the distinctive theology of Qumran. It also included fragments of *Tobit* (in Aramaic and Hebrew), of *Ecclesiasticus* (in Hebrew) and of the

Letter of Jeremiah (in Greek).[1] Were these works, which large tracts of the Christian Church were to venerate as deuterocanonical (*i.e.*, in the second grade of canonicity), venerated in any such way at Qumran? We cannot say with certainty, for the mere fact of their presence among the Qumran fragments provides no evidence one way or the other.

A book may be authoritative in a religious community without being given the status of a divine oracle. The *Book of Common Prayer* is an authoritative document in the Church of England, but it is not part of Holy Writ. The *Rule of the Community* was an authoritative document at Qumran, but no one suggests that it was regarded as canonical scripture. *Jubilees* was also an authoritative document at Qumran; the community apparently accepted the solar calendar of Jubilees as that instituted by God in the beginning (Gen. 1: 14), and it is very probably referred to in the *Zadokite Work* as "the book of the divisions of times into their jubilees and weeks." But was it regarded as canonical in the sense of being divinely inspired? We cannot as yet give a confident answer to this question.

Daniel was clearly a favourite book with the Qumran sectaries, and may well have enjoyed canonical status among them. Two copies of this book have been identified from Cave 1, four from Cave 4 and one from Cave 6. These follow the traditional Hebrew text, apart from a few variant readings related to the Hebrew text presupposed by the Septuagint version. Fragments from Caves 1 and 4 have preserved the two places in Daniel where the language changes—from Hebrew to Aramaic in 2: 4 and back from Aramaic to Hebrew in 8: 1. No further light is thrown by the Qumran finds thus far on the problem of the two languages in Daniel.

The deuterocanonical additions to Daniel (*Susanna, Bel and the Dragon*, the *Prayer of Azariah* and the *Song of the Three Young Men*) have not been identified at Qumran. It appears from these additions that the cycle of stories about Daniel continued to grow after the publication of the canonical book,[2] and indeed we can recognize among these additional stories a variant account of one of the canonical incidents (Daniel's six days' imprisonment in the lions' den in the story of *Bel and the Dragon* is patently a variant of the incident narrated in chapter 6). And even the canonical book has been thought to have "the appearance rather of a series of excerpts than of a continuous narrative, and the hypothesis that the present book is an abridgment of a larger work (partly

---

[1] See p. 28.

[2] Josephus adds a story, not otherwise known, about Daniel's building a tower at Ecbatana in Media (*Antiquities* x. 11. 7).

preserved in its original language and partly translated) has much in its favour."[1]

Alongside the fragments of the canonical Daniel found at Qumran fragments have also been found of one or more Daniel cycles not represented in either the canonical or deuterocanonical documents. One of these fragments, the *Prayer of Nabonidus*, written in Aramaic, represents that king as telling how he was afflicted with a sore inflammation for seven years "in the city of Teman," and how, when he confessed his sins, he received help from one of the Jewish exiles in Babylon. This may well be a variant of the story of Nebuchadnezzar's madness in Daniel 4, but it is attached to another Babylonian king, Nabonidus (556–539 B.C.), and preserves a reminiscence of his historical residence at Teima in North Arabia. Further fragments of a Daniel cycle, also in Aramaic, represent Daniel as rehearsing events of Biblical history from the Deluge and the Tower of Babel down to Hasmonean times, and going on from there to predict what is to happen in the end-time.

These discoveries may not add to our knowledge of the history of the Old Testament canon, but further study of them may illumine a number of the literary problems of the book of Daniel.

Literary Criticism

When the first news of the discoveries was released, their main significance was felt to lie in the new light which they might be expected to throw upon the text of the Old Testament. The reason for this has already been mentioned. If it was indeed true, as the first scholars to examine the scrolls claimed, that they belonged to the early years A.D., or the closing centuries B.C., then we had Hebrew Biblical manuscripts nearly a thousand years nearer to the time at which the Old Testament books were written than the earliest that were previously known. When further evidence seemed to confirm the early dating of the scrolls, a number of questions were eagerly asked. The first scroll to receive much publicity, and the first to be published in facsimile, was the complete manuscript of Isaiah from Cave 1. What fresh information could it supply about the problems arising from the study of that particular book? Did it prove, for example, that there were not "two Isaiahs," but one only?

To this question the scroll 1 Q Isaiah A[2] gives no answer which

---

[1] C. H. H. Wright, *An Introduction to the Old Testament* (1891), pp. 193 f.

[2] It has proved convenient to distinguish Qumran manuscripts according to the particular caves where they were found by the use of the symbols 1 Q (*i.e.*, from Qumran Cave 1), 4 Q (*i.e.*, from Qumran Cave 4), etc.

THE SCROLLS AND THE OLD TESTAMENT 59

could tell us more than was known already. Even if it was copied
out as early as 175 B.C., we knew that by that time the Book of
Isaiah was current in practically its present form. For around the
year 180 B.C. the Jewish sage Jesus Ben-Sira wrote his book of
wisdom which we know as Ecclesiasticus; and in the section of
that book entitled "The Praise of the Fathers," which celebrates
the memory of great Israelites of earlier days, he makes it plain
that the Book of Isaiah as known to him ran on at least to what we
call Chapter 61. Speaking of King Hezekiah, who reigned in
Judah during part of Isaiah's lifetime, Ben-Sira says (Ecclus.
48: 22–25):

> For Hezekiah did what was pleasing to the Lord,
>   and he held strongly to the ways of David his father,
> which Isaiah the prophet commanded,
>   who was great and faithful in his vision.
> In his days the sun went backward,
>   and he lengthened the life of the king.
> By the spirit of might he saw the last things,
>   and comforted those who mourned in Zion.
> He revealed what was to occur to the end of time,
>   and the hidden things before they came to pass.

In these lines Ben-Sira quotes indiscriminately from all parts of
the Book of Isaiah. The reference to Isaiah's "vision" probably
echoes Isa. 1: 1; the reference to the sun's going backward and
the adding of life to the king recalls the story of Hezekiah's sickness in Isa. 38; the prophet's seeing "the last things" may be an
allusion to Isa. 2: 2; his comforting "those who mourned in Zion"
is a combined reference to Isa. 40: 1 and 61: 3; and the last two
lines of the quotation from Ben-Sira hark back to such passages
as Isa. 41: 4, 22 f., 26 and 48: 6. So there is nothing surprising in
the fact that a manuscript of Isaiah written rather later in the same
century should contain the material of all sixty-six chapters, as
1 Q Isaiah A does.

As soon as complete facsimiles of this scroll were available,
many people looked up the place where Chapter 39 ends and
Chapter 40 begins, and were impressed to find that there is no
space between the two. In fact, Chapter 40 begins on the last
line of a column. But this proves nothing. Those who think it
does should be on their guard, lest they be invited to apply their
own argument to an earlier part of the scroll. For Chapter 33
comes to an end near the foot of a column where there is still
room for three lines of writing. But Chapter 34 does not begin
immediately below the last line of Chapter 33; the space at the
foot of the column is left blank, and Chapter 34 begins at the top

of the following column. But has it ever been suggested that there is a change of authorship at the end of Chapter 33? Yes, indeed. In his lectures on *The Prophets of Israel*, for example (written in 1882), William Robertson Smith quoted the closing verses of Chapter 33 as containing the last message of "First Isaiah." "And so Jehovah's word to Isaiah ends, as it had begun," he says, "with the forgiveness of sins." But actually it would be as unsafe to argue that the space after Chapter 33 indicates a change of authorship there as it would be to argue that the absence of a space after Chapter 39 excludes a change of authorship there. The space after Chapter 33 might indicate rather a change of scribe, or it might have been left if a scribe copied the first half of the book from one manuscript and the second half from another. In brief, the scroll tells us nothing at all about the stages by which our Book of Isaiah took its present form; and the only reason for dwelling on the matter at such length is that it has been suggested (even by people who ought to have known better) that this scroll gives a decisive answer to all our questions about the literary criticism of the book.

But certain theories of a few literary critics do seem to be put out of court by the scroll. One or two sections of Isaiah have been dated by some scholars in the Maccabean age—i.e. in the years following 168 B.C. One scholar thought that the portrayal of the Suffering Servant owed its inception to the suffering of the pious Jewish martyrs under Antiochus Epiphanes at that time;[1] another dated Chapters 24 to 27 (the so-called "Isaiah Apocalypse") in the reign of John Hyrcanus (135–104 B.C.).[2] It is certain that, if these extreme theories were well founded, these sections of Isaiah could never have been included in a manuscript of the book written about the middle of the second century B.C. But what are we to say of a scholar of our own time, who in the course of a study of the Dead Sea Scrolls found it possible to suggest that the portrayal of the Suffering Servant was based on the experience of the Teacher of Righteousness, whose death he placed between 67 and 63 B.C.?[3]

Let us leave these questions of literary criticism, and turn to textual criticism, on which 1Q Isaiah A and the other Biblical manuscripts discovered at Qumran and Murabba'at have something more positive to say.

[1] R. H. Kennett, *The Servant of the Lord* (1911).

[2] B. Duhm, *Das Buch Jesaia* (1892).

[3] See A. Dupont-Sommer, *The Dead Sea Scrolls* (1952), p. 96. When reference is made to Professor Dupont-Sommer's earlier studies in the scrolls, it should be remembered that they were preliminary and provisional in character; he has now produced a magisterial and definitive work in *Essene Writings from Qumran* (Eng. trans., 1961).

The Biblical Text

How do these earlier Biblical texts compare with those which we had hitherto known as the earliest surviving ones? Did the Jewish scribes who copied the sacred books generation after generation during the first nine centuries of the Christian era do their work accurately or carelessly? Did they introduce many mistakes? Do the newly discovered scrolls enable us to make large-scale corrections in the Massoretic manuscripts?

The new evidence confirms what we had already good reason to believe—that the Jewish scribes of the early Christian centuries copied and recopied the text of the Hebrew Bible with the utmost fidelity. Their workmanship was much more accurate than the workmanship of the Christian scribes who copied and recopied the text of the Greek Bible.

The text of 1Q Isaiah A became available just in time for the translators of the Revised Standard Version of the Old Testament to make use of it before that version made its public appearance in September, 1952. Dr. Millar Burrows, who was a member of the Revision Committee, tells us[1] that thirteen readings in all were adopted in which 1Q Isaiah A deviates from the traditional text, and he adds that in some cases where he voted for the adoption of these readings he now thinks the traditional text ought to have been retained after all. One place where they were certainly right in adopting the reading of 1Q Isaiah A was in Isa. 21 : 8, where the RSV says (in reference to a watchman who is looking out for the arrival of a messenger across the Syrian desert from the east): "Then he who saw cried: 'Upon a watchtower I stand, O Lord . . .'" There, by an accidental interchange of consonants, the Massoretic text has introduced the quite irrelevant figure of a lion, so that the AV reads, "And he cried, 'A lion . . .'" while the RV reads, "And he cried as a lion . . ."

Again, in the RV Isa. 14 : 4 appears in the form: "How hath the oppressor ceased! the golden city ceased!" The word translated "golden city" is an odd one, and the revisers of 1884 were not too sure about its meaning; in the margin they suggested "exactress" as an alternative rendering. But it could have one or the other of these meanings only if it were derived from the Aramaic (not Hebrew) word for "gold." In the RSV the rendering is: "How the oppressor has ceased, the insolent fury ceased!" For the rendering "insolent fury" the new revisers are able to appeal to the Greek, Syriac and Latin versions, and also to one ancient Hebrew manuscript. This manuscript is 1Q Isaiah A, which, by

---

[1] *The Dead Sea Scrolls* (1955), pp. 304 ff.

exhibiting the letter *r* where the traditional Hebrew text has the very similar letter *d*, yields a meaning in essential agreement with that found in the three ancient versions.

In Isa. 60: 19 1Q Isaiah A adds the expression "by night" to the second clause, thus completing the parallelism between the two clauses. Similarly the RSV renders: "The sun shall be no more your light by day; not for brightness shall the moon give light to you by night" (where the traditional Hebrew text, followed by the older English versions, lacks "by night").

But there is one place where we might certainly have expected the RSV to adopt a reading of 1Q Isaiah A—and there, remarkably enough, it has not even mentioned it in a footnote. In the oracle of the Suffering Servant in Chapter 53, verse 11 begins in the Massoretic text with the words which AV and RV render: "He shall see of the travail of his soul, and shall be satisfied." Now the Septuagint, the pre-Christian Greek translation of the Old Testament, adds the noun "light" as an object in the first clause of this verse, and it has generally been surmised that the Hebrew text originally had this word, but that it dropped out inadvertently in the course of copying and recopying. Critical editions of the Hebrew text regularly have a footnote at this point suggesting that the original reading was "From (or 'after') the travail of his soul he will see *light*, he will be satisfied." And this provides an answer to the reader's natural question when he considers the verse in the Massoretic text: "*What* will he see?" But now there is no need merely to *surmise* that the Hebrew text originally included the word "light"; it is there, plain for all to see, in the oldest known Hebrew manuscript—1Q Isaiah A. And, as if that were not enough, it is present in the incomplete Isaiah manuscript which was also found in Cave 1—1Q Isaiah B. There is no close relation between these two manuscripts, apart from the fact that they were stored in the same cave; and the fact that both have the word "light" in Isa. 53: 11 is exceedingly strong evidence that this is the original text. Yet the RSV strangely ignores this reading, and offers instead a paraphrase of the Massoretic text: "he shall see the fruit of the travail of his soul and be satisfied."

Another very attractive reading of 1Q Isaiah A which the RSV does not mention is in Isa. 40: 12, where we find "Who has measured *the waters of the sea* (Hebrew *mê yam*) in the hollow of his hand?" instead of the Massoretic "Who has measured *the waters* (Hebrew *mayim*) in the hollow of his hand?"

1Q Isaiah A bears all the marks of a popular, unofficial copy of the sacred text. It was probably the work of amateur scribes, or at least of scribes who did not belong to the higher grades of their profession. The spelling is much more phonetic than the classical

Hebrew spelling. Hebrew writing consisted originally of consonants only; the small dots and dashes which serve as vowel-points were not devised until the eighth and ninth centuries A.D. But at quite an early date some of the letters of the Hebrew alphabet (all of which had as their primary function the representation of consonantal sounds) were used for the secondary function of indicating certain important vowel-sounds. This use of vowel-letters appears as early as the inscription of Mesha, king of Moab, on the Moabite Stone (c. 850 B.C.), and readers of the Hebrew Bible are quite familiar with it. But it appears on a greatly extended scale in 1Q Isaiah A, and this was probably intended to help people who (unlike the regular readers in synagogues) were not expert in reading Hebrew. It has even been suggested, very reasonably, that the nationalist revival of Maccabean days probably promoted a renewal of interest in Hebrew as the traditional Jewish language, which had been displaced for many generations as a vernacular by the related Aramaic tongue. Jews who were trying to learn Hebrew afresh, like Zionists of more recent times, would naturally be glad of a more phonetic spelling than was practised in the schools.

For this reason 1Q Isaiah A throws incidental light on the pronunciation of Hebrew in Palestine in the second century B.C. Another minor respect in which it deviates from the traditional text is in certain grammatical forms and endings. An English analogy to this kind of deviation will be found if we compare forms like "saith" in the AV with "says" in the RSV. Here, too, the scroll provides some interesting information on the evolution of Hebrew inflexions. But deviations in spelling and accidence, of course, make no difference to the meaning, and disappear in the course of translation. Most of the deviations in 1Q Isaiah A which do make a difference to the meaning of the text—additions, omissions, and alterations of words and groups of words—simply show, when subjected to critical scrutiny, that the text of this manuscript, ancient as it is, is not so accurate as the traditional text which was received and handed on by the Massoretes.

As for 1Q Isaiah B, the differences between its text and that of the Massoretes are fewer and less significant. Whereas 1Q Isaiah A was probably copied by the eye (that is to say from an earlier copy lying before the scribe or scribes), 1Q Isaiah B appears to have been copied by the ear (that is to say, someone read aloud from an older manuscript and the scribe wrote down what he heard, or what he thought he heard). Some of the scribal slips in 1Q Isaiah B are plainly due to faulty hearing. He found difficulty, for example, in distinguishing between the various guttural sounds in Hebrew. But he produced a much neater and more accurate piece of work than 1Q Isaiah A, which is rather slovenly by comparison. And, so far as the general impression made by the text of 1Q Isaiah B is concerned, it is as close to the traditional Massoretic text as makes no practical difference. That is one reason why its exhibition of the word "light" in Isa. 53: 11 is so noteworthy; clearly that word was present in the Hebrew text in general use at the beginning of the Christian era, and was dropped by accident at some point between then and A.D. 400 (it was absent from the Hebrew text on which Jerome based his Latin translation of the Old Testament at the beginning of the fifth century).

We have reason to believe, then, that the consonantal text of the Hebrew Bible which the Massoretes edited had been handed down to their time with conspicuous fidelity over a period of nearly a thousand years. There is some evidence that the text was revised about the beginning of the second century A.D. by Rabbi Aqiba and his colleagues, who wished to see an authoritative text uniformly accepted by the Jewish people. But the testimony of these two manuscripts, which belong to a period earlier than Aqiba's generation, shows that the revising and editing which these scholars undertook cannot have involved any significant modification of the sacred writings. Perhaps they were concerned to exclude some eccentric texts which were in circulation, but in so far as they fixed a standard form, it was the form which was already widely accepted as standard.

We know that during the attack which was launched by Antiochus Epiphanes on the religious life of the Palestinian Jews in 168 B.C., the sacred scriptures were seized and destroyed by the king's officers. "The books of the law which they found they tore to pieces and burned with fire. Where the book of the covenant was found in the possession of any one, or if any one adhered to the law, the decree of the king condemned him to death" (I Macc. 1: 56 f.). It was inevitable, then, that when religious freedom was regained by the Jews a few years later, there should be an urgent call for new copies of the sacred books to replace those that were destroyed; not only would fresh copies be made but others would be imported from Jewish colonies outside Palestine. And while the exact course of events in this regard cannot be reconstructed, it appears quite probable that the form of text which the Massoretes inherited through the intervening generations from Aqiba and his contemporaries went back beyond their time to the Maccabean age.

As more and more copies of Hebrew Scripture were discovered at Qumran and Murabba'at and published for the benefit of the world of Biblical learning, it became evident that the Massoretic text was not the only form represented among them. The text of the Old Testament has come down to us along three main lines of transmission. One of these is the Massoretic line which has already been referred to. Another line is represented by the Greek translation called the Septuagint. We have excellent manuscripts of the Septuagint belonging to the fourth century A.D., very substantial fragments belonging to the century before that, and smaller fragments of even earlier date,[1] the earliest being four fragmentary columns of a papyrus roll of Deuteronomy in Greek which was written in the second century B.C. It is well known that, when all allowances have been made for freedom and even inaccuracy in translation and for the use of paraphrase and interpretation in preference to a literal rendering of several passages, the Hebrew text from which the Septuagint version was made differed in many particulars from the traditional Hebrew text which has been handed down to us. It is natural to assume that the Septuagint version was based on copies of the Hebrew Bible which were current in Egypt (more especially, in Alexandria) in the last three centuries B.C., for it was primarily for the use of the Greek-speaking Jewish community of Alexandria that the Septuagint was produced. But it is only since the Qumran discoveries that copies of *Hebrew* Scripture have come to light which show readings formerly known only from the *Greek* Old Testament, and recognized as characteristic of the Septuagint.

Nor is that all. There was a third line of transmission along which one division of the Hebrew Bible was preserved. The Samaritans have preserved the Hebrew text of the Pentateuch in a recension of their own which goes back to the time when the breach between them and the Jews became final, shortly before the end of the period of Persian domination in the fourth century B.C. And some Hebrew Biblical texts found at Qumran have closer affinities with the recension hitherto regarded as distinctively Samaritan than with that which has been handed down in the Jewish tradition.

The conlusion to which we are forced is this: that all three forms of text—the Hebrew text received and transmitted by the Massoretes, the Hebrew text underlying the Septuagint, and the Hebrew text of the Pentateuch preserved by the Samaritans— were in no sense sectarian in the closing centuries of the Second Jewish Commonwealth, but were varying types of text current among the people of Israel in general, including the Jews of Palestine. It may be that the Massoretic text goes back to a Babylonian recension, while the Septuagint was based on the Hebrew text current in Egypt and the Samaritan was a Palestinian

---

[1] In addition to more recent Septuagint discoveries from the Dead Sea region (see pp. 28, 34).

E

text. In any case, whatever differences might exist between the Qumran covenanters and their fellow-Jews (not to mention the Samaritans), it is certain that they shared the same Biblical texts. If three distinguishable types of text were used at Qumran, that was because they were used elsewhere in Palestine. But the later remains found at Murabba'at and its neighbourhood show only one type of Bible text in Hebrew. That is the Massoretic type, and the reason may well be that Aqiba and his colleagues had by this time established the Massoretic type as the one to be accepted, rather than the other two types represented at Qumran. And if Aqiba and his colleagues did in fact establish the Massoretic form of text as authoritative, we must applaud their sound judgment; for in the majority of places where one of the other forms deviates from the Massoretic reading, the Massoretic reading is superior.

When the Biblical fragments discovered by the archaeological explorers of Qumran Cave 1 in 1949 were studied, it was announced that a Hebrew fragment of Deuteronomy exhibited a reading in Ch. 31: 1 ("And Moses finished speaking all these words") which agreed with the Septuagint and not with the Massoretic text (which reads: "And Moses went and spoke these words"). But much more evidence of the same kind was forthcoming when the fragments from Cave 4 began to be examined. The best preserved Biblical document from Cave 4 is a Hebrew copy of the Books of Samuel. This scroll originally comprised fifty-seven columns, of which forty-seven have now been identified. This Hebrew text of Samuel is very much the type of text which the Septuagint translator of Samuel must have used. More remarkable still, it bears a close affinity to the text of Samuel which the author of the Books of Chronicles must have used in the composition of his work—closer than to the text of Samuel preserved in the Massoretic tradition.

A Hebrew fragment of Exodus agrees with the Septuagint against the Massoretic text by giving seventy-five instead of seventy as the number of Jacob's descendants in Ex. 1: 5 (compare Acts 7: 14).

A tiny fragment of Deut. 32: 8 exhibits for the first time documentary evidence for a Hebrew reading which has long been inferred on the basis of the Septuagint. In the Massoretic text this verse runs (as in the RV):

When the Most High gave to the nations their inheritance,
When he separated the children of men,
He set the bounds of the peoples
According to the number of the children of Israel.

The Septuagint reading of the last phrase is: "according to the number of the angels of God." From this it was concluded that the Hebrew text used by the Septuagint translator here did not have "children (sons) of Israel" but "sons of God" (in the sense in which that expression is used in Gen. 6: 2, 4; Job 1: 6; 2: 1; 38: 7). Many went further and regarded this as a preferable reading to that of the Massoretic text. Thus the RSV renders the last phrase "according to the number of the sons of God," mentioning in a footnote that this is the reading implied by the Greek version, while the Hebrew has "Israel" and not "God." But now one fragmentary Hebrew manuscript can be cited in support of the reading "sons of God."

Another Hebrew fragment from Cave 4 preserves part of the middle of this chapter (the "Song of Moses") and presents readings which were previously known only from the Septuagint: for example, in verse 15 "But Jeshurun waxed fat and kicked" is amplified to "But Jacob ate and waxed fat, and Jeshurun kicked"; and in verse 19 "the LORD saw it, and was moved to jealousy" appears in place of the Massoretic reading, "the LORD saw it, and spurned them."

The end of Deut. 32 exhibits in the Septuagint some marked divergencies from the Massoretic text. In particular, verse 43 is twice as long in the Septuagint version (and it is from a clause in the Septuagint of this verse which is absent from the Massoretic text that the words "Let all the angels of God worship him" are quoted in Heb. 1: 6). Another Hebrew fragment of Deut. 32 from Cave 4 runs from verse 37 to verse 43 and presents readings like those in the Septuagint which had not been found previously in any Hebrew manuscript.

Of the prophetical books, it is Jeremiah that shows the greatest divergence between the Septuagint and Massoretic texts. The Septuagint text of this book is appreciably shorter than the Massoretic text. The shorter text is exhibited in a Hebrew copy of Jeremiah from Cave 4, but the longer text is also represented among the Biblical manuscripts from Qumran.

From Cave 4 comes a fragmentary scroll of the Book of Exodus in palaeo-Hebrew script which exhibits a type of text hitherto regarded as distinctively Samaritan. One of the distinctive features of the Samaritan Pentateuch is a persistent tendency to expansiveness. For example, if Moses is told to do something (for example, in connexion with the succeeding plagues of Egypt in the earlier chapters of Exodus), the Samaritan version is not content to say that "Moses did so"; it must go through all the details again as they are listed in the instructions given to Moses, and record how Moses carried them out one by one. Again, in the early chapters of Deuteronomy Moses rehearses in the first person a good part of the narrative of Exodus, but here and there in Moses' retrospect details are added which are absent from the traditional text of Exodus; the Samaritan text inserts these in the appropriate contexts of Exodus. But these and other features formerly regarded as typically Samaritan are found in this scroll from Cave 4. We are not bound to suppose that there was any special contact between the Qumran community and the Samaritans (although such contact has been inferred on other grounds); what this and similar discoveries[1] mean is that there was a time when this form of text was not peculiar to the Samaritans, but was current among Jews of Palestine as well. The Samaritan text is in essence a popular Palestinian recension of the traditional text.

The Biblical manuscripts proper are not the only Qumran documents which provide us with the information about the Biblical text. The Biblical commentaries are also useful in this respect, the more so because the commentators make skilful use of textual variants. Where one variant suits a commentator's purpose better than another, he will use it, although his exposition may show plainly that he is well aware of an alternative reading. Out of several instances that might be given, let one suffice, from the commentary on Habakkuk found in Cave 1.

The Massoretic text of Hab. 2: 16, as rendered in the RV, runs: "Thou art filled with shame for glory: drink thou also, and be as one uncircumcised. . . ." For "be as one uncircumcised," however, the Septuagint and Syriac, by a simple transposition of two Hebrew letters, render "stagger"; and this is the basis of the RSV rendering, "Drink, yourself, and stagger!" But now it appears that the Qumran commentator read "stagger" in his Biblical text, for he quotes the first part of verse 16 in this form. But when he comes to give his exposition of the words, he indicates that he was acquainted with the alternative reading, "be as one uncircumcised," for he combines both ideas in his application of the prophet's denunciation to the Wicked Priest, the inveterate enemy of the community: "Its interpretation concerns the priest whose shame was mightier than his glory, for he did not circumcise the foreskin of his heart but walked in the ways of drunkenness to quench his thirst."

In addition to texts which can be classified quite distinctly as related to one or another of these three families (corresponding to the Massoretic, Septuagint and Samaritan editions) there are others which exhibit a mixture of features of two or more of these families, and it may be that some belong to other families which have not yet been identified. Thus we have a manuscript of

[1] For another Samaritan reading see p. 82.

Numbers from Cave 4 whose text is midway between the Samaritan and Septuagint types, while a manuscript of the books of Samuel from the same cave (not the one mentioned on p. 66) has been thought to exhibit a text superior to the Massoretic and Septuagint texts alike. It will be a long time before a clear picture of the position is obtainable. But in general the new discoveries have increased our respect for the Massoretic Hebrew text. In a number of places it calls for emendation (the readings "he who saw" in Isa. 21: 8, "light" in Isa. 53: 11, and "sons of God" in Deut. 32: 8 are highly probable emendations); but over the whole area of the Old Testament writings its superiority to the other forms of text current at the end of the pre-Christian era is assured. The "great, indeed all-important question" which Sir Frederic Kenyon asked in 1939 is well on the way to receiving a much more explicit and positive answer than was thought possible then: "Does this Hebrew text, which we call Massoretic, and which we have shown to descend from a text drawn up about A.D. 100, faithfully represent the Hebrew text as originally written by the authors of the Old Testament books?"[1]

[1] *Our Bible and the Ancient Manuscripts*, 4th edn., p. 47.

CHAPTER VII

BIBLICAL INTERPRETATION

ANOTHER question about the Qumran community's relation to the Old Testament leads us right into the heart of
the community's life and faith. How did they *interpret* the
Old Testament?

They interpreted it in such a way as to see their own duty in
the perilous times through which they lived written clearly there
for their instruction. This is immediately evident from one of
the first scrolls to be unrolled—the Habakkuk commentary from
Cave I.[1] We have already seen how they reinterpreted the
situation in which Habakkuk found himself, and saw in his words
a description of their own circumstances.

There has never been any lack of people who have treated the
Biblical prophecies in this way. In our own day we have seen
how earnest Bible students thought they recognized in Hitler or
Stalin the embodiment of the Antichrist foretold in the New
Testament. In the early nineteen-thirties a gentleman in England,
who edited a short-lived periodical to give currency to his highly
individual interpretations of the Bible, published copies of letters
which he had written to Mussolini and Einstein, informing them
that they were respectively the Beast and the False Prophet—two
sinister eschatological figures in the Book of Revelation. (Einstein
sent him a brief and courteous reply—which was duly published—to the effect that if the Biblical writers could have fore-
seen the interpretations which would one day be put upon their
words, they might have thought twice before setting pen to paper!)
And throughout the Christian era there have been serious people
who believed, generation after generation, that their own days
were the days of fulfilment, when history was to be wound up.

Our commentator, living some decades before the beginning of
the Christian era, was sure that the time of the end was fast
approaching, and that Habakkuk and the other prophets had

---

[1] It must not be assumed that all the non-Biblical writings found at Qumran
reflect the community's beliefs and practices. These writings (with the Biblical
documents accompanying them) are the remains of the community's library,
and no community would like it to be supposed that all the books in its library
could be used as sources of information about its life and thought. But many
of the non-Biblical works from Qumran do represent a self-consistent system
of belief and practice, distinct from that of the main streams of Judaism, and
in the light of other literary and archaeological evidence can reasonably be
used to reconstruct the outlook and fortunes of the Qumran community.

prophesied primarily of the days which had now set in. Therefore he set himself to study and apply the words of Habakkuk according to what he believed to be their true meaning. That
meaning was inevitably vague and mysterious until the time of
fulfilment arrived; with its arrival, the meaning was plain for those
who had eyes to see and hearts to understand. So he quotes the
prophecy of Habakkuk, section by section, and adds the interpretation to each section as he goes along. Here is a sample of
his method:[1]

(Hab. 1: 4) *So the law is slacked.*—The interpretation of this is
that they have rejected the law of God.

And justice never goes forth, for the wicked surrounds the righteous.—
The interpretation of this is that "the righteous" is the Teacher of
Righteousness and "the wicked" is the Wicked Priest . . .

(1: 5) *Look among the nations, and see; wonder and be astounded:
for I am doing a work in your days that you would not believe if told.*—
The interpretation of this concerns wicked and deceitful men, with
the Man of Falsehood, because they did not believe that which the
Teacher of Righteousness had told them from the mouth of God;
and it concerns those who acted deceitfully against the commandments of God and against the new covenant, because they did not
believe in the covenant of God and did not keep His holy sabbath.
And so the interpretation of the matter concerns those who act
deceitfully in the latter days, violent men who break the covenant,
who will not believe when they hear all that is coming upon the last
generation from the mouth of the priest into whose heart God has
put wisdom, to interpret all the words of His servants the prophets
through whom He foretold what was to come upon His people and
upon His land.

(1: 6) *For lo, I am rousing the Chaldeans, that bitter and hasty
nation.*—The interpretation of this concerns the Kitti'im, who are
fleet and mighty in battle . . .

And so our commentator goes on; every sentence in the prophecy of Habakkuk is made to yield some reference to the two
contrasted figures, the Wicked Priest and the Teacher of Righteousness, with their followers and associates, or else to the ruthless
Kitti'im, who are sent by God to execute His judgment upon the
oppressive rulers of His people, but who behave even more
oppressively than those whom they put down.
Since the Kitti'im are plainly a world-power, pursuing a career
of conquest and empire from the west, it may be thought that we

---

[1] Here and there in this "sample" a gap in the text has been filled in.

shall have greater success in identifying them than in identifying Jewish individuals who, for all the importance which the commentator attached to them, may not have left their mark on the pages of history. Further details are given of their irresistible terror as the commentator explains how Habakkuk was really describing them when, to a superficial view, he was describing the Chaldeans of his own day.

These Kitti'im, then, in their swift advance, overthrow all who stand in their way, and subdue them to their own dominion. They take possession of many lands and plunder the cities of the earth, "to seize habitations not their own," as Habakkuk says (1 : 6). Nor do they rely on military power alone to accomplish their ends: "with deliberate counsel all their device is to do evil, and with cunning and deceit they proceed with all the nations" (this is a comment on 1 : 7). "They trample the earth with their horses and their animals; they come from afar, from the islands of the sea, to devour all the nations vulture-wise, and they are never satisfied" (this on 1 : 8). "With wrath and anger, with hot passion and fury, they speak to all the nations" (this on 1 : 9). They mock at kings and potentates; they scoff at a mighty host; they laugh at fortresses, for they surround them with a large army and terrorize the defenders into surrender. This, too, is a sign of divine justice; these strongholds are surrendered because of the iniquity of those who dwell in them (all this is by way of a comment on 1 : 10). Yet these Kitti'im have rulers who follow one another in quick succession; "they come one after another to destroy the earth" (this on 1 : 11).

When Habakkuk describes the Chaldeans as netting men like fish (1 : 15), the commentator explains that the Kitti'im "gather their wealth with all their plunder like the fish of the sea." And when the prophet goes on to say that the Chaldeans thereupon pay divine honours to the nets in which they have taken their captives (1 : 16), the commentator says that the Kitti'im sacrifice to their standards and regard their weapons of war with religious veneration. They impose heavy tribute on the nations, to be paid year by year, thus denuding the lands of their wealth. And in war they are completely pitiless: their sword spares neither men, women, nor the tiniest children.

It is difficult to avoid the conclusion that these Kitti'im are the Romans. Several of the individual points in the description would be applicable to other conquerors, but the whole impression can scarcely be said to fit any other conquering people of whom we know. Alexander's invasion of Asia is too early for other elements in the picture, and cannot be related to several details in the description of the Kitti'im. His successors, the Ptolemies and

Seleucids, who battled in Palestine did not come from "the islands of the sea" but from Egypt and Syria.[1] The rulers of the
Kitti'im, who followed one another in quick succession, "by the
counsel of a guilty house" (perhaps a reference to the Roman
senate), may remind us of the chief magistrates of Rome, elected
annually to serve for a year; or we may recall that in the Near
East, during the first century B.C., one Roman commander-in-
chief was displaced by another with disconcerting suddenness and
frequency. While the statement that the Kitti'im pay divine
honours to their standards and weapons may be a rhetorical
exaggeration, it is a fact that the "eagles" and other standards of
the Roman army were regarded as sacred objects. The "eagle,"
the standard of a legion, was kept in a special shrine in the military
camp and was regarded as affording sanctuary. When the legion-
aries under Titus stormed the Jerusalem temple in A.D. 70,
Josephus describes how they set up their standards over against
the eastern gate and offered sacrifices to them there. The Seleucids
may have had a similar practice, but the evidence in their case is
ambiguous and scanty as compared with that for the Romans.

At one time it was thought that in another of the scrolls from
Cave 1, the *Rule of War*, where the term Kitti'im also occurs, the
reference must certainly be to the Seleucids and the Ptolemies,
because a distinction was made between the Kitti'im of Assyria
and the Kitti'im in Egypt. But when the complete scroll was
published, this interpretation no longer seemed so inevitable, for
the "Kitti'im of Assyria" could reasonably be understood of the
Roman administration of Syria and the "Kitti'im in Egypt" of
the Roman forces in Egypt, the more so as the *Rule of War* appears
to have been composed after the Roman occupation of Judæa,
perhaps in the Herodian period[2].

But the reference to the *Rule of War* gives us a further opportunity of illustrating the belief of the Qumran community that
they were living in the last days, and that all the things foretold
by the prophets were due to be fulfilled in the very near future.

As they read the prophets, they gathered that the last days were
to be marked by a final and decisive conflict, of unprecedented
bitterness, between the forces of right and the forces of wrong.

[1] The Seleucid kings are indeed said to have hired mercenaries from these
islands (the expression is used especially of the Aegean archipelago and coasts),
but these were foreign troops, additional to their regular forces (I Macc. 6:
29; 11: 38). In I Macc. 15: 1 "the islands of the sea" appears as a conventional
phrase where the island of Rhodes is actually in question.

[2] In that case "the king of the Kitti'im in Egypt" mentioned in the *Rule of
War* might be Mark Antony, in the years between 41 and 31 B.C. The Romans
had no "king" in the strict sense, but Orientals could well give the title to a
man who wielded more than royal power and who, if not himself a king, was
at any rate a king-maker.

In Chapters 38 and 39 of Ezekiel, for example, they read of an invasion of Palestine from the north, led by one Gog, ruler of the land of Magog. Gog would march at the head of a vast international host, which would be annihilated by divine intervention. Probably when Alexander the Great marched south along the Syro-Palestinian coastal road from Asia Minor some Jewish thinkers identified him with Gog, but the event proved them wrong. But this time, surely, the identification could not be in doubt!

Again, as they read the Book of Daniel, they read in the closing verses (36–45) of Chapter 11 about a self-willed king from the north who would establish dominion over Egypt, Libya and the Sudan, and then turn back from there to pitch his camp with hostile intent west of Jerusalem; "yet he shall come to his end, with none to help him." Those days would be days of un-paralleled affliction for the faithful in Israel, and they would owe their deliverance to the intervention of Michael the archangel as their champion.

The men of Qumran believed firmly that these days of un-paralleled affliction were imminent. The last warfare of all was about to break out—the struggle, as they called it, "of the sons of light against the sons of darkness." But, even if they could expect Michael to arise as their champion and bring them final victory, they must not remain passive in this critical hour; they must go forth to the help of the Lord against the mighty. To do this effectively they must study the art of war. And the results of their study are set down in the *Rule of War*. In the twentieth chapter of Deuteronomy they found regulations for the ancient institution of the holy war in Israel; these, they decided, must be brought up to date and put into practice, for the expected battle was not theirs, but the Lord's. The military technique of those far-distant days when their ancestors invaded Canaan under the leadership of Joshua, however, would not be adequate for the situation in which the men of Qumran now found themselves. Accordingly, they set themselves to study the contemporary art of war, with the aid of the most up-to-date Roman military manuals, such as Herod the Great may have adapted for the training of his soldiers.[1] With this remarkable combination of ancient religion and modern technique they prepared to sustain a forty years' war. (But, in accordance with the ancient law of holy war, they would abstain from hostilities every seventh year.)

---

[1] Some scholars have dated the *Rule of War* in the Hellenistic period; notably K. M. T. Atkinson, "The Historical Setting of the 'War of the Sons of Light and the Sons of Darkness'", *Bulletin of the John Rylands Library* 40 (1957–58), pp. 272 ff. But the battle order described in the *Rule* bears a much closer resemblance to that of the Romans in the first century B.C. than it does to the Macedonian phalanx.

At an early stage in the war they would return from "the wilderness of the peoples" where they lived in exile to encamp in "the
wilderness of Jerusalem" and give battle to the Kitti'im and their
allies. After the overthrow of these enemies, they would deal
with the Kitti'im in Egypt, and the dominion of the Kitti'im
would disappear completely. A pure sacrificial worship would
be restored in Jerusalem, under acceptable priests. The warfare would be continued against other "sons of darkness"—the
ancestral enemies of Israel in seven of the surrounding lands.
There would be seven major campaigns; in three of these the
sons of light would conquer and in three they would be vanquished,
but the seventh time final victory would be secured for them
through the intervention of Michael. The men of Belial would
be annihilated; the triumph of the people of God, foretold by so
many of the prophets of old, would be achieved; everlasting
righteousness would be brought in; the kingdom of heaven would
be established in perpetuity. In words which echoed the ancient
victory-songs of Old Testament and Maccabean times they sang
in advance the chant of welcome with which the conquering hero,
the captain of the Lord's host, would be received after his victory
over the sons of darkness:

> Arise, O mighty man, and lead thy captivity captive, thou man of
> glory!
> Gather thy plunder, O thou who doest valiantly!
> Set thy hand on the necks of thy foes
> And thy foot on the heaps of the slain!
> Smite through the nations, thy adversaries,
> And let thy sword devour the flesh of guilty man.
> Fill thy land with glory,
> And thy heritage with blessing;
> Let there be a multitude of cattle in thy camps,
> Silver and gold and precious stones in thy palaces!
> O Zion, rejoice exceedingly;
> Break forth with ringing shouts, O Jerusalem;
> And be joyful, all ye cities of Judah!
> Open thy gates continually,
> That they may bring into thee the wealth of nations,
> And their kings may serve thee;
> All who have oppressed thee shall pay thee homage
> And lick the dust of thy feet.
> O daughters of my people, sing with a voice of ringing joy;
> Deck yourselves with ornaments of glory and beauty!

In a commentary on Isaiah from Cave 4, the Assyrian advance
and downfall of Isaiah 10: 22 ff. are interpreted of the eschatological "war of the Kitti'im." The leader of the Kitti'im (or so it
appears, for the document is sadly mutilated) goes up from the

plain of Acco to the boundary of Jerusalem. Then follows a quotation of Isaiah 11: 1–4, which is (very properly) interpreted of the "shoot of David," the Davidic Messiah, who is to arise in the latter days to rule over all the Gentiles, including "Magog," but takes his directions from the priests.[1] This is in line with the general messianic expectation cherished at Qumran, in which the priesthood is envisaged as taking precedence over the Davidic Messiah, whose main function is to lead his people to victory in battle.

A fragmentary commentary on Micah from Cave 1 provides a good example of allegorical interpretation. Here the words, "What is the transgression of Jacob? Is it not Samaria?" (Mic. 1: 5), are interpreted of "the Prophet of Falsehood, who leads astray the simple," while the following words, "And what are the high places of Judah? are they not Jerusalem?", are interpreted of "the Teacher of Righteousness, who teaches the law to his people and to all those who offer themselves to be gathered in among God's elect, practising the law in the council of the community, who will be saved from the day of judgment." The Teacher of Righteousness we know; the Prophet of Falsehood is evidently the leader of a rival sect—the Pharisees, in my opinion. But the only way of reading these two rival leaders out of Micah's reference to the transgression of Jacob and the high places of Judah is first of all to read them in—by arbitrary allegorization.

Considerable portions have survived of a commentary on Psalm 37 from Cave 4. Here "those who wait for the LORD," those who "shall possess the land" (verse 9), are "the congregation of His elect who do His will"—i.e. the Qumran community. The "little while" after which "the wicked will be no more" (verse 10) is the probationary period of forty years at the end of the age, comparable to the probationary period of forty years in the desert in Moses' day.[2] At the end of the eschatological period of forty years "there will not be found in the earth any wicked man" (how the wicked are to be got rid of in just that period is explained in greater detail in the *Rule of War*). "The wicked," who "draw the sword and bend their bows, to bring down the poor and needy" (verse 14) are "the wicked ones of Ephraim and Manasseh who will seek to put forth a hand against the priest and the men of his counsel in the time of trial which is coming upon them." The "priest" is almost certainly the Teacher of Righteousness.[3] But he and his followers will not be left to the mercy of their enemies; "God will

---

[1] See p. 87.

[2] *Cf.* the New Testament application of the "forty years" of Ps. 95: 10 in Heb. 3: 7 ff. See also pp. 74, 96.

[3] *Cf.* the comment on Hab. 1: 5, quoted on p. 71.

redeem them from their hand, and afterwards they (the wicked) shall be given into the hand of the terrible ones of the Gentiles for judgment." There is a further possible reference to the Teacher of Righteousness in the comment on verses 32 f. ("The wicked watches the righteous, and seeks to slay him. The LORD will not abandon him to his power, or let him be condemned when he is brought to trial"); but the comment unfortunately is very defective: "Its interpretation concerns the Wicked [Priest] who sent [to the Teacher of Righteousness (?)] to kill him . . . and the law which he sent to him. But God will not abandon him to his power, or let him be condemned when he is brought to trial". But if the commentator did see a reference to the Teacher of Righteousness in this passage (which, on the analogy of Qumran interpretation of similar passages, is highly probable), the Wicked Priest's attempt to slay the Teacher seems to have been unsuccessful, for his deliverance is mentioned here as in the comment on verse 14.

The interpretation of Old Testament scripture exhibited by the Qumran commentaries and related documents is based upon the following principles:

(a) God revealed his purpose to His servants the prophets, but this revelation (especially with regard to the time of the fulfilment of His purpose) could not be properly understood until its meaning was made known by God to the Teacher of Righteousness, and through him to his followers.

(b) All that the prophets spoke refers to the time of the end.

(c) The time of the end is at hand.

These principles are put into operation by the use of the following devices:

(a) Biblical prophecies of varying date and reference are so interpreted as to apply uniformly to the commentator's own day and to the days immediately preceding and following—that is, to the period introduced by the ministry of the Teacher of Righteousness and the emergence of the eschatological community of the elect.

(b) The biblical text is atomized so as to bring out its relevance to the situation of the commentator's day; it is in this situation, and not in the natural sequence of the text, that logical coherence is to be looked for.

(c) Variant readings are selected in such a way as best to serve the commentator's purpose.[1]

(d) Where a relation cannot otherwise be established between the text and the situation to which it is believed to refer, allegorization is pressed into service.

[1] See p. 68.

It has, of course, become a major preoccupation of students of the Qumran literature to interpret the Qumran commentaries so as to elucidate their historical and personal references. The difficulty of doing so may be gauged by the great variety of solutions proffered. One source of difficulty is that leading personalities are denoted by descriptive titles rather than by personal names. Many a religious minority will venerate a Teacher of Righteousness, complain of persecution at the hands of a Wicked Priest, and despise the easy-going majority as Seekers after Smooth Things, followers of a Prophet of Falsehood. Even the Gentile power which looms so largely in the literature is mentioned allusively as the Kitti'im, a term which in itself might denote either Greeks or Romans.

There is, however, one fragmentary commentary which actually refers to historical characters by name. This is a commentary on Nahum from Cave 4, which explains the prophet's description of Nineveh as a lions' den (2: 11) as a reference to "[Deme]trius, king of Greece, who sought to enter Jerusalem by the counsel of the Seekers after Smooth Things." The personal name is unfortunately mutilated, but it can scarcely be anything but Demetrius. We have a choice between three Seleucid kings of that name—Demetrius I (162–150 B.C.), who sent Nicanor to seize Jerusalem at the instigation of the high priest Alcimus and his supporters; Demetrius II (145–139/8 B.C.), who sent a force against Jonathan; Demetrius III (95–88 B.C.), who invaded Judæa at the invitation of hostile Jewish subjects of the Hasmonean king Alexander Jannaeus (103–76 B.C.). The "Seekers after Smooth Things," who are mentioned in other places in Qumran literature,[1] are best identified with the Pharisees, who led the opposition to Jannaeus throughout most of his reign.

The comment on Nahum 2: 11 continues: "[Never has that city been given] into the hand of the kings of Greece from Antiochus to the rise of the rulers of the Kitti'im, but ultimately it will be trodden down . . ." This Antiochus may well be Sidetes, whose demolition of the walls of Jerusalem early in the reign of John Hyrcanus (135–104 B.C.) was the last effective action by a Gentile ruler against the city until Pompey entered it in 63 B.C. In that case the Demetrius mentioned in the previous sentence of the commentary will surely be Demetrius III. It may also be pointed out that the reference in this context to "the rulers of the Kitti'im"

---

[1] They may have received this name because their application of the law was less rigorous than that adopted by the Qumran community; but we may also detect an echo of Isa. 30: 10, where the prophet's hearers say to him: "speak to us smooth things, prophesy illusions."

makes the identification of the Kitti'im with the Romans practically certain.

Nahum 2: 12 goes on: "The lion tore enough for his whelps, and strangled prey for his lionesses; he filled his caves with prey, and his dens with torn flesh." In these words the commentator sees a reference to "the raging lion, who smote with his mighty ones and the men of his counsel" and "took vengeance on the Seekers after Smooth Things, in that he proceeded to hang them up alive [which was never done] in Israel before, for concerning one hung up alive on a tree the Scripture says. . . ." What the Scripture says is that such a person is "accursed by God" (Deut. 21: 23); but our scribe evidently could not bring himself to pen such ill-omened words. In any case, the Scripture envisages the hanging of a dead body on a tree; the Qumran commentator on Nahum has something more dreadful in mind—hanging men up alive, in other words, crucifying them. That "such a thing was never done in Israel before" means that it had never been done by an Israelite. We know that Jewish confessors were crucified by Antiochus Epiphanes, but the first Jewish ruler to punish his enemies in this way, so far as we know, was Jannaeus. These enemies were his rebellious subjects who invited Demetrius III to help them to overthrow him. The revolt did nearly succeed, but when Alexander at last was able to crush it, he took a ghastly revenge on those of its leaders on whom he could lay hands. "As he feasted with his concubines in the sight of all the city," says Josephus, "he ordered about eight hundred of them to be crucified, and while they were still living ordered the throats of their wives and children to be cut before their eyes."[1] The lesson was not lost on those of his opponents who were still at large. About eight thousand of them fled by night, and remained in exile during the remainder of his reign. The identity of the "raging lion" is almost as certain as if he had been explicitly named.

The Nahum commentary, then, provides us with more certain criteria for relating Qumran exegesis to history than we find in the other commentaries published to date. And these criteria may, with due caution, be used to throw light on ambiguous references in other Qumran texts. The Qumran commentaries plainly do not give us much help in understanding the Old Testament. But the serious student of Scripture can never fail to be interested in what was thought of its meaning by serious students of earlier days; and in this regard the Qumran commentaries on the Old Testament have opened a new world for our exploration.

[1] *Antiquities* xiii. 14. 2.

CHAPTER VIII

THE MESSIANIC HOPE

WE know that in certain forms of Jewish expectation the final victory over the enemies of Israel and the establishment of the kingdom of God was closely associated with a Messiah. The term "Messiah," let us remind ourselves, means "Anointed One"; and anyone who is so designated holds his office "by divine right" or "by the grace of God." Thus even a pagan monarch like Cyrus could be addressed as the "Messiah" of the God of Israel (Isa. 45: 1) because he had been raised up in order to fulfil God's purpose, and by his policy and activity he was energetically promoting that purpose, however little he was aware of the fact. But the title is given pre-eminently to the kings of David's dynasty, and in later times was used of an expected ruler of that dynasty who would restore and surpass the vanished glories of David's imperial days.

What light do the Qumran texts throw on Israel's messianic hope? In what form was it cherished within the Qumran community?

We have already mentioned[1] a fragmentary commentary on Isaiah from Cave 4 in which the prophecy of "a shoot from the stump of Jesse" in Isa. 11: 1 ff. is interpreted of the "shoot of David who is to arise in the latter days." This is, of course, the Messiah of David's line, whose world-wide dominion is foretold.

From the same cave comes a compilation of *Patriarchal Blessings*, in which Jacob's blessing on his son Judah (Gen. 49: 10) is expounded thus:

> *A ruler shall not depart from the tribe[2] of Judah.*—When dominion comes for Israel [there shall never] fail an enthroned one therein for David. For the "ruler's staff"[3] is the covenant of kingship, and the "feet" are the families of Israel.

> *until he come* who is the rightful Messiah, the shoot of David, for to him and to his descendants has been given the covenant of kingship over his people for everlasting generations.

[1] See pp. 75 f.

[2] "Tribe" and "sceptre" are denoted by the same word in Hebrew; this quotation paraphrases the Massoretic text, which, as rendered in the RSV, runs: "The sceptre shall not depart from Judah."

[3] *Cf.* the second line of Gen. 49: 10, RV and RSV: "nor the ruler's staff from between his feet" (AV has "a lawgiver" instead of "the ruler's staff"; the Hebrew word here is capable of either meaning).

The words which follow are mutilated, but it is clear that they bring the expected Messiah into relation with the Law and with the "men of the community." What is of chief importance is that Jacob's blessing of Judah is here regarded as a prediction of the coming of the Davidic Messiah (David belonged, of course, to the tribe of Judah). The enigmatic word "Shiloh" (*cf.* AV and RV) is paraphrased as "the rightful Messiah" (literally, "the Messiah of righteousness"). With this we may compare the RSV rendering, "until he comes to whom it belongs" (*cf.* Ezek. 21: 27, "until he comes whose right it is," which probably echoes Gen. 49: 10).

Yet another document from Cave 4 (4Q *Florilegium*) is an anthology of passages referring to the glorious prospects awaiting the house of David. In the following extract from it, the prophet Nathan's promises to David about the perpetuity of his dynasty are coupled with a prophecy at the end of the Book of Amos about the future restoration of David's dynasty:

> *The* LORD *declares to you that he will build you a house; and I will raise up your seed after you, and I will establish the throne of his kingdom for ever. I will be his father, and he shall be my son* [II Sam. 7: 11–14].
> —This is the shoot of David, who is to arise with the Expounder of the Law . . . in Zion in the latter days, as it is written:

> *And I will raise up the booth of David that is fallen* [Amos 9: 11].
> —That is David's fallen booth, but he will arise hereafter to deliver Israel.[1]

Once again we have clear evidence of the Qumran community's expectation of the anointed prince of the house of David. There is nothing sectarian about this expectation, although it is possible that the community looked for this prince to arise from its own ranks. When the Qumran documents make a straightforward reference to "the Messiah" in the singular, it is this Davidic prince that is meant. The "Expounder of the Law" with whom the Messiah is to arise in the latter days, according to this last passage we have looked at, will receive further mention.[2] For this is not the only Qumran text to suggest that when the Messiah appears, he will not be unaccompanied.

In the *Rule of the Community* it is laid down that the community in question shall continue to live under its original rule

---

[1] Both these passages are quoted in the New Testament: the former in Heb. 1: 5, where it is used to set Jesus forth as the Son of God, and the latter in Acts 15: 15–18, where the promise of the rebuilding of David's fallen booth is seen to be fulfilled in the Gentile mission of the Church, through which people of many nations yield allegiance to Jesus, "great David's greater Son".

[2] See pp. 85, 87 f.

F

"until the coming of a prophet and the anointed ones (Messiahs) of Aaron and Israel" (column 9, line 11).[1] These are presumably figures whose advent is expected to mark the epoch for which the community was making preparation. Further light is thrown upon this expectation by the contents of a document found in Cave 4, evidently written in the earlier part of the first century B.C. by the scribe to whom we owe the copy of the *Rule of the Community* found in Cave 1.

This brief document, commonly known as 4Q *Testimonia*, brings together a few passages from the Old Testament which formed the basis for certain "messianic" expectations. It begins with the Samaritan text of Ex. 20: 21b, which represents a combination of the common text of Deut. 5: 28–29 and 18: 18–19, the latter being the place where God says to Moses: "I will raise up for them [*i.e.* for the people of Israel] a prophet like you from among their brethren." Next comes a quotation from Num. 24: 15–17, where the Mesopotamian prophet Balaam foresees the rise of a military conqueror in Israel (probably King David):

> I see him, but not now;
> I behold him, but not nigh:
> a star shall come forth out of Jacob,
> and a sceptre shall rise out of Israel;
> it shall crush the forehead of Moab,
> and break down all the sons of Sheth.

This is followed by the blessing pronounced by Moses upon the tribe of Levi (the priestly tribe) in Deut. 33: 8–11, which begins with the words:

> Give to Levi thy Thummim,
> and thy Urim to thy godly one.[2]

The document closes with a section dealing with a completely different subject, at which we shall look later on.[3]

The way in which these three quotations are brought together suggests that the writer looked forward to the advent of a great prophet, a great captain or prince, and a great priest. And this threefold expectation is certainly related to the words already quoted from the *Rule of the Community*. The expected prophet is

---

[1] The section which ends with these words is absent from an earlier copy of the *Rule*, found in Cave 4.

[2] The Thummim and the Urim constituted the oracular equipment by means of which the chief priest in ancient Israel ascertained the divine will.

[3] See pp. 90 f.

obviously common to both; as for the "anointed ones of Aaron and Israel," these can readily be identified with the two other figures envisaged in the collection of Biblical quotations—the great priest being the "Messiah of Aaron" and the great prince the "Messiah of Israel" (identical in all probability with the Davidic Messiah).

In this connexion it is interesting to note that one of the names by which the community described itself was the community of Israel and Aaron (*i.e.* laymen and priests). And it probably expected both the Messiah of Israel and the Messiah of Aaron to emerge from its own ranks.

In the two parts of the *Zadokite Work*—the *Admonition* and the *Laws*—several references are made to the "Messiah of Aaron and Israel" who was expected to arise in the end of the days. This expression in itself could denote either one Messiah or two, but in the light of these other references in the Qumran texts it probably denotes two—the priestly and lay Messiahs.

In ancient Israel two outstanding offices were "messianic" in the sense that men were appointed to these offices by the solemn ceremony of anointing. These were the priesthood and the kingship. The king of Israel was known as "the LORD's anointed," but the priest (more especially the chief priest) was also known as "the anointed." To both is accorded the Hebrew designation *mashiach* (Messiah), which is translated in the Septuagint, the Greek version of the Old Testament, as *christos* (Christ). Both priest and king were in their varying ways mediators between God and their people, and so was the prophet, although he was not regularly installed in his prophetic office by anointing. (Elijah's command, in I Kings 19: 16, to anoint Elisha to be prophet in his place is exceptional.) Even the prophets, however, could be described collectively as God's anointed men, because they acted under His commission, even if no oil had been poured on their heads. Thus, in God's charge with regard to the patriarchs in Psa. 105: 15—

> Touch not my anointed ones,
> do my prophets no harm!—

the parallelism shows that "anointed ones" (Messiahs) and "prophets" are synonymous terms. And there are a couple of places in the Zadokite *Admonition* and one in the *Rule of War* where the expression "anointed ones" appears with the evident meaning of "prophets."

In any case, we have found an interesting point of contact between Qumran and Christianity—a point of contact which is also a point of cleavage. The Qumran community and the early Christians agreed that in the days of the fulfilment of all that the Old Testament prophets had said there would arise a great prophet, a great captain and ruler, and a great priest. But these three figures remained distinct in Qumran expectation, whereas the early Christians saw them unified in the person of Christ. The threefold office of Christ as Prophet and Priest and King, a well-established theme in traditional Christian theology, is implicit in various early strands of New Testament teaching.

It is worth while, however, to look at the three passages quoted on the leaf from Cave 4 in the light of the early Christian interpretation of the Old Testament.

The Prophet

The first quotation, the passage about the prophet like Moses whom God would raise up, is referred to several times in the New Testament. According to John 1: 21, a deputation which came from Jerusalem to interview John the Baptist during his baptismal ministry in the Jordan valley asked him if he claimed to be one or another of the various figures who were expected to arise in Israel at the time of fulfilment. Was he the Messiah? Was he Elijah (who was expected to return to earth shortly before the Messiah appeared)?[1] But when he assured them that he was neither the Messiah nor Elijah, they asked him, "Are you the prophet?" And he answered, "No." He did not need to ask, "Which prophet?" He knew at once which prophet they meant—the prophet of whom Moses spoke in Deut. 18: 15 ff.

The same Evangelist tells us that when Jesus had fed the multitude with loaves and fishes by the Sea of Galilee, the people said: "This is indeed the prophet who is to come into the world!" (John 6: 14). They linked the food with which Jesus had just fed them with the manna which their forefathers ate in the wilderness in the days of Moses: surely this must be the new prophet, the second Moses! And when Jesus stood in the temple court at the Feast of Tabernacles and invited the thirsty to come and drink, the people said, "This is really the prophet" (John 7: 37 ff.), for they remembered how Moses had fetched water from the rock for their forefathers to drink in the wilderness. Again, when three of Jesus' disciples saw the vision of Jesus in glory along with Moses and Elijah, on the mount of transfiguration, they heard a heavenly voice directing their attention to Jesus: "This is my beloved Son; listen to him" (Mark 9: 7). Those words, "listen to him," echo the words of Moses in Deut. 18: 15 ("The

[1] See p. 140.

LORD your God will raise up for you a prophet like me from among you, from your brethren—*him you shall heed*") and mark Jesus out as the prophet whom Moses had in mind.

This identification of Jesus with the prophet like Moses finds even more explicit expression in the early chapters of the Book of the Acts: once in Acts 3: 22, where Peter, in the court of the Jerusalem temple, quotes the actual words of Moses from Deut. 18 and refers them to Jesus, and once in Acts 7: 37, where Stephen, on trial for his life before the Sanhedrin, quotes the same words as a prediction of Jesus.

The Prince

Balaam's prophecy about the star out of Jacob was plainly a favourite with the Qumran community. It appears not only on the leaf from Cave 4, but also in two major community documents. In the Zadokite *Admonition* (column 7, lines 19 f.) the "star" and the "sceptre" (which in the original oracle are variant symbols for one and the same figure) are dissociated: the "star" is "the Expounder of the Law" (probably the anointed priest of the new age),[1] but the "sceptre" is "the prince of all the congregation," that is to say, the military leader. The oracle is also interpreted of the military leader in the *Rule of War* (column 11, line 6), in the course of a hymn of thanksgiving to God: "Thine is the warfare; from thee is the strength; it is not ours, it is not our might or the power of our hands that has wrought valiantly, but by thy might and the strength of thy great valour, even as thou hast made it known to us from of old, saying: 'A star shall come forth out of Jacob, and a sceptre shall rise out of Israel . . .'" Here the conquest foretold in the oracle is identified with the expected victory over the Kitti'im and other sons of darkness.

This passage from Num. 24: 17 does not figure among the messianic prophecies applied to Jesus in the New Testament (unless there is a distant allusion to it in the title "the bright morning star" in Rev. 22: 16). But it was soon seized upon by Christians as one of the scriptures which bore witness to Him. Thus the Christian apologist and philosopher Justin Martyr, in his *Dialogue with Trypho the Jew* (Chapter 106), says: "And that He [Jesus] should arise like a star from the seed of Abraham, Moses showed beforehand when he said: 'A star shall arise out of Jacob, and a leader from Israel.'" Justin's citation of these words was the more significant at the time (*c*. A.D. 135), for Trypho had lately escaped from the disastrous fighting in Palestine which followed Rabbi Aqiba's recognition of the messianic claimant

[1] See p. 87.

Simeon Ben-Kosebah as the "star out of Jacob" (whence his new patronymic Bar-Kokhba).[1] So Num. 24: 17 was interpreted of the Messiah by a leader in the main stream of Jewish tradition as well as by the Qumran covenanters and the Christians.

If, however, the New Testament writers did not invoke the Balaam oracle as a prophecy fulfilled by Jesus, they did apply to Him other Old Testament passages which similarly depict a mighty conqueror. Outstanding among these are Psa. 2 and 110. In the former of these the Davidic king, the LORD's anointed, says:

> I will tell of the decree of the LORD:
> He said to me, "You are my son,
>   today I have begotten you.
> Ask of me, and I will make the nations your heritage,
>   and the ends of the earth your possession.
> You shall break them with a rod of iron,
>   and dash them in pieces like a potter's vessel."

In the latter the psalmist addresses the king thus:

> The Lord is at your right hand;
>   he will shatter kings on the day of his wrath.
> He will execute judgment among the nations,
>   filling them with corpses;
> he will scatter chiefs
>   over the wide earth.[2]

Such passages could be applied quite literally in the Qumran documents to the valiant hero who would lead the faithful to victory in the war against the sons of darkness; that the early Christians could apply them to Jesus shows how thoroughly (under His influence, of course) they had transmuted their military significance. After all, the most convinced Christian pacifists of our day sing quite cheerfully hymns like *Onward! Christian soldiers* and *Fight the good fight* because the warfare to which these words refer is waged against spiritual enemies. We may wonder idly what some archaeologist of two thousand years hence will make of a fragment of Sankey's hymn-book when he finds the first hymn in the collection opening with these words:

> Ho, my comrades! see the signal
>   Waving in the sky!
> Reinforcements now appearing;
>   Victory is nigh!

---

[1] See pp. 32 ff.

[2] These particular words from Psa. 110 are not quoted in the New Testament, but the priest-king to whom they are addressed is repeatedly identified with the Christian Messiah (cf. Mark 12: 36; Acts 2: 34 f.; I Corinthians 15: 25; Heb. 1: 13; 5: 6, etc.).

We can imagine what ludicrous mistakes he may well make; but are we making similarly ludicrous mistakes in our interpretation of the Qumran *Rule of War*? Probably not; for the *Rule of War* is mainly prose, not poetry; and the military language seems too direct and circumstantial to be allegorical.

The Priest

As for the passage from Deut. 33 which our document from Cave 4 quotes as forecasting a priestly Messiah, this chimes in with a number of other texts from Qumran which indicate quite clearly that, while the community certainly expected the Davidic Messiah to arise and pursue his victorious career for the deliverance of Israel at the end-time, they also expected the emergence of an anointed priest, who would be head of the state in the new age and from the Davidic Messiah would receive his orders.

The "mighty man" of the *Rule of War* might well be the expected "Messiah of Israel" but alongside him in the *Rule of War* there stands the high priest, who is apparently his superior. Similarly, in a collection of benedictions discovered in Cave 1, a blessing for the high priest and one for the other priests are followed by a blessing for the "prince of the congregation." And in another document from the same cave, entitled the *Rule of the Congregation*,[1] the order of precedence is laid down for a banquet which appears to have its setting in the new age. The Messiah of Israel is there—in fact he is said to be "brought" (if not indeed "begotten") by God[2]—but he occupies a subordinate place to the priest. "Let no one begin to eat bread or drink wine before the priest, for it is his province to bless the first mouthful of bread and wine and to stretch forth his hands first upon the bread. Thereafter the Messiah of Israel may stretch forth his hands upon the bread." This reminds us forcibly of the subordinate position of the Davidic "prince" to the priesthood in the programme for the new commonwealth set out in the last nine chapters of the Book of Ezekiel; in fact, there is good reason to believe that the men of Qumran hoped to put Ezekiel's programme into effect when the proper time came.

It is the great priest, the head of state in the new commonwealth, who is referred to as the "Expounder of the Law" in two documents at which we have looked (see pp. 81, 85). In both of these places this "Expounder of the Law" appears in close

---

[1] A companion document to the *Rule of the Community*, but distinct from it.

[2] The manuscript seems quite clearly to read "when [God] *begets* (Heb. *hôlîd*) the Messiah (or 'causes the Messiah to be born') with them" (for which expression we might compare Psalm 2: 7), but this may be a scribal error for "when [God] brings (Heb. *hôlîk*) the Messiah with them."

association with the Davidic Messiah of the end-time, "the prince of the congregation". But why should the priest be called the "Expounder of the Law"? Because "the lips of a priest should guard knowledge, and men should seek the law (or 'instruction', Heb. *torah*) at his mouth, for he is the messenger of the LORD of hosts" (Mal. 2: 7). If this is true, or at any rate ought to be true, of priests in general, then the Messiah of Aaron under whom the ideal constitution of the people of God would be realized should surely be the Expounder of the Law *par excellence*.[1]

Before we leave this subject of the priestly Messiah in the Qumran texts, it should be mentioned that in one interesting work, which scholars nowadays are inclined to associate fairly closely with the Qumran movement (though it can scarcely be called a community document) a notable part in the victory and restoration of the last days is ascribed to a Messiah of the tribe of Levi, who stands alongside the Messiah of the tribe of Judah and indeed overshadows him. This work is *The Testaments of the Twelve Patriarchs*, a pre-Christian Jewish treatise which has come down to us in a Christian recension. The significance of its Levitical Messiah is, however, uncertain; some have thought that here we have a reflection of the conditions of the Hasmonean period, when supreme power in Israel was exercised by a priestly family.[2]

Neither Moses' blessing of the tribe of Levi nor any other Old Testament mention of the Levitical priesthood is applied to our Lord in the New Testament. The reason is not far to seek; one New Testament writer expresses it succinctly when he says: "it is evident that our Lord was descended from Judah, and in connexion with that tribe Moses said nothing about priests" (Heb. 7: 14). He could not be hailed as a "Messiah of Aaron." No one in apostolic times, so far as we can gather, ascribed to Him a priestly heritage on the ground that His mother was related to the mother of John the Baptist, who was "of the daughters of Aaron" (Luke 1: 5)—although this argument was brought forward at a later date. There is some evidence, indeed, that certain Jewish Christians denied the legitimacy of the Jerusalem priesthood and regarded James the Just and other members of the holy family as the true high priests of the new Israel; but this was not based on any claim to Aaronic descent but on their relationship

[1] The title "Expounder of the Law" is also given in the *Zadokite Work* to a historic figure associated with the community; see pp. 93, 96.

[2] It has been widely held that in its original form this work spoke of a Levitical Messiah only, and that its references to a Messiah of the tribe of Judah are later (Christian?) interpolations; but more probably both Messiahs figured in the *Testaments* from the beginning. Fragments of earlier recensions of the *Testament of Levi* (in Aramaic) and the *Testament of Naphtali* (in Hebrew) have been found in the Qumran caves. See pp. 154 f.

to Jesus. But when the New Testament ascribes a priestly status to Jesus, it does so on totally different grounds. The writer of the Epistle to the Hebrews finds Old Testament authority for the priestly side of Jesus' messianic work in Psa. 110: 4, where a prince of the house of David is hailed by God as "a priest for ever after the order of Melchizedek." There was sound historical justification for ascribing a priesthood of this order to the Davidic Messiah, for it is extremely probable that after David's capture of Jerusalem he and his successors viewed themselves as heirs to the ancient royal priesthood exercised by Melchizedek and other pre-Israelite rulers of that city. The writer to the Hebrews does not dwell on this historical basis for his argument (perhaps he was not greatly interested in it); but by developing the doctrine of Jesus' perpetual priesthood in terms of the Old Testament portrayal of Melchizedek he has given the Christian Church its classic exposition of this phase of our Lord's messianic dignity and service.

The Qumran community, then, had its messianic doctrine. One point in which it differs from the messianic doctrine of the New Testament, as we have said, is its expectation of three distinct personages at the end of the age, whereas the Christian Messiah is Prophet and Priest and King in one. But there is a more important point of difference than that. There is a constant danger of confusion when we use the term "Messiah," because in the Christian tradition our ideas of what is meant by it are determined by the life and work of Jesus. But in fact His life and work have quite changed the meaning of the term. It was no doubt because of the meaning which was popularly attached to it by those among whom He moved that Jesus Himself, except on rare and significant occasions, did not make use of it. His hearers would have been misled if He had done so. He knew Himself to be Messiah-designate from the moment of His baptism, if not before. But from the same moment, if not before, He also knew that His Messiahship must be fulfilled in terms of the obedient and suffering Servant of the Lord. The messianic figures whom we meet in the Qumran documents do not achieve their destiny in this manner. There was indeed a most moving interpretation of the Servant Songs accepted by the Qumran community, but it does not appear to have influenced the way in which they envisaged the great messianic figures of the end-time. But all the phases of our Lord's messianic ministry receive their distinctive quality from the historical figure of the Son of Man, who came not to be served by others but to be a Servant Himself, and to give His life a ransom for many.

APPENDIX: CONCERNING A SON OF BELIAL

We may now look at the final section of the Testimony document which points forward to the prophet, prince and priest of the end-time, although this final section makes no contribution to our knowledge of the community's messianic doctrine. The personage of whom it speaks is more of an Antichrist than a Christ.

When Joshua had finished praising and giving thanks in his praises, he said: "Cursed be the man who builds this city: at the cost of his firstborn shall he lay its foundation, and at the cost of his youngest son shall he set up its gates". And behold, an accursed man, one of the sons of Belial, shall arise, to be a very sna[re of the f]owler to his people, and destruction to all his neighbours. And he shall arise and [make his sons] rulers, [so that] they two may be instruments of violence. And they shall build again the . . . [and s]et up a wall and towers for it, to make a stronghold of wickedness . . . in Israel, and a horrible thing in Ephraim and Judah, . . . [and they shall w]ork pollution in the land, and great contempt among the sons of . . . [and shall shed b]llood like water on the rampart of the daughter of Zion, and in the boundary of Jerusalem.

This passage is said to be an extract from a work called the *Psalms of Joshua*, which is independently attested among the Cave 4 material. It is not strictly a commentary, but the passage quoted above certainly follows the principles of the Qumran commentators in its interpretation of Joshua's curse on the rebuilder of Jericho (Josh. 6: 26).

According to the Massoretic text, Joshua said, "Cursed before the LORD be the man that rises up and builds this city, Jericho." It may be that the word "Jericho" was absent from the Qumran author's copy of Joshua (as it is from the Septuagint), but the context makes it clear that Joshua was referring to Jericho. It is not certain, however, that the Qumran author applied the curse to a rebuilding of Jericho; he may have had another incident in mind, such as one of the successive fortifications of Jerusalem; conceivably, but improbably, he may have intended the "city" in a metaphorical sense.

If, however, we look for a man with two sons, all in positions of authority, who take a leading part in the rebuilding of a Judæan city, and cause great bloodshed in the precincts of Jerusalem, we have an embarrassing wealth of choices. F. M. Cross says that "the application of the passage to Simon and his older and younger sons Judas and Mattathias, and their deaths in Jericho is almost too obvious to require comment. The slaughter in Jerusalem and its environs described in the last lines reflects the attack of Antiochus Sidetes upon Judæa in 134–132 B.C. immediately following Simon's death."[1] But the application is not so obvious to many other scholars. J. T. Milik[2] prefers to think of Mattathias (father of the Maccabees) and his two sons Jonathan and Simon, both of whom took part in the rebuilding of Jerusalem's fortifications.[3] (The reference to Jerusalem at the end of the passage does at least suggest that it, and not Jericho, is the city whose rebuilding the commentator has in mind.) But the idea that the pious Mattathias should be described as "one of the sons of Belial" makes one lift an eyebrow, to say the least.

If we pass other members of the Hasmonean family in review, we may think of Jonathan, whose two sons were unsuccessfully sent to Trypho as hostages for their father's release[4]; of John Hyrcanus and his two sons Aristobulus I and Alexander Jannaeus;[5] of Jannaeus and his two sons Hyrcanus II and Aristobulus II; or even of Aristobulus II and his two sons Alexander and Antigonus. Since 4Q Testimonia is said to be the work of a scribe who wrote in the earlier part of the first century B.C., the last of these identifications is ruled out on palaeographical grounds. The same grounds may also be held to rule out the identification of the parties concerned with Jannaeus and his two sons. Jannaeus may be more notorious for destroying cities than for building them; but the palaeographical evidence should be carefully scrutinized before we dismiss an interpretation which would recognize the civil strife between Hyrcanus II and Aristobulus II, with the consequent intervention of the Romans, as the occasion of the bloodshed around Jerusalem. But at least this may serve as an example of the difficulty of correlating the Biblical exegesis of Qumran with events in the relevant period of Jewish history.

[1] *The Ancient Library of Qumran and Modern Biblical Studies* (1958), p. 113. For Simon's death cf. I Macc. 16: 11 ff.; for the subsequent investment of Jerusalem by Antiochus VII cf. Josephus, *Antiquities* xiii. 8. 2.

[2] *Ten Years of Discovery in the Wilderness of Judaea* (1959), pp. 63 f.

[3] I Macc. 10: 10 f.; 13: 10; 14: 37.

[4] I Macc. 13. 16 ff.

[5] In view of the Samaritan affinities of 4Q *Testimonia* in Biblical text and interpretation, the identification of the son of Belial with John Hyrcanus might be thought very appropriate; he was an object of special execration to the Samaritans because he destroyed their temple on Mount Gerizim. He fortified Jerusalem and built the tower of Baris N.W. of the temple. He is also said to have predicted the misfortunes of his two sons Aristobulus and Jannaeus. It should be added that the identification of the son of Belial is quite unconnected with the identification of the Wicked Priest.

CHAPTER IX

THE TEACHER OF RIGHTEOUSNESS
AND HIS ENEMIES

A COMPREHENSIVE scheme of Biblical interpretation such as the Qumran community followed is not likely to have arisen by accident. It bears the impress of an original mind, and we are told quite plainly whose mind this was.

THE TEACHER IN THE COMMUNITY DOCUMENTS

The Zadokite *Admonition* tells how a righteous remnant of the people of Israel, probably in the second century before Christ, realized that they were involved in the general national apostasy, and decided to renew the ancient covenant with the God of their fathers. But for some time they were uncertain what course of life they should adopt in order to maintain their loyalty to the covenant. After twenty years, however, God raised up a "Teacher of Righteousness" who taught them the true way of life. Not only so, but this Teacher of Righteousness was given special insight into the purpose of God, so that he was able to make known to the "last generations" what God was going to accomplish in the "last generation." And it was evidently to the Teacher of Righteousness that our community owed its distinctive interpretation of Old Testament prophecy, as well as its organization by camps like a miniature Israel in the wilderness, its rigorous discipline and its expectation of the near advent of the day of the Lord.

With this agrees much of what is said about the Teacher of Righteousness in the Habakkuk commentary found in Cave 1. As we have seen, the warnings of judgment in Habakkuk's oracle are directed by the commentator against those who refuse to believe "that which the Teacher of Righteousness had told them from the mouth of God." And when the commentator goes on to denounce those covenant-breakers "who will not believe when they hear all that is coming upon the last generation from the mouth of the priest into whose heart God has put wisdom, to interpret all the words of His servants the prophets through whom He foretold what was to come upon His people and upon His land," we naturally understand by the "priest" either the Teacher of Righteousness in person or else (less probably) someone who perpetuated his interpretation of Scripture after his decease. In one place in the *Zadokite Work* the Teacher of Righteousness (for it can hardly be anyone else) is referred to as "the Expounder of the Law" who took a leading part among those "who turned from impiety in Israel and went out of the land of Judah and sojourned in the land of Damascus" (*i.e.* the wilderness retreat of the community); and we have already seen how suitable a title "the Expounder of the Law" would be for a priest who discharged his duties faithfully.[1]

In Hab. 2: 1–2 the prophet describes how, in his perplexity to comprehend the purpose of God, he determined to wait for the further light that might come with the unfolding of God's purpose in history, and received a fresh assurance from God that the final vindication of righteousness would not be long delayed. "I will take my stand to watch, and station myself on the tower, and look forth to see what he will say to me, and what I will answer concerning my complaint. And the LORD answered me: 'Write the vision; make it plain upon tablets, so he may run who reads it. . . .'" Here is the commentator's interpretation of this passage:

> God told Habakkuk to write the things that were to come upon the last generation, but the fulfilment of the appointed time He did not make known to him. And as for the words, "so that he may run who reads it," their interpretation concerns the Teacher of Righteousness, to whom God made known all the mysteries of the words of His servants the prophets.

That is to say, Habakkuk was enabled to foresee what was going to happen in the end-time, but he was not told when the end-time would arrive. But when the Teacher of Righteousness arose, God revealed to him that the end-time was at hand, and showed him how the predictions of Habakkuk and the other prophets were about to be fulfilled. For, it was believed, all the prophets had spoken of the end-time rather than of their own days. If Isaiah, for example, announced the downfall of the enemy of the people of God in the words, "And the Assyrian shall fall by a sword, not of man; and a sword, not of man, shall devour him" (Isa. 31: 6), he was not so much referring to the overthrow of Sennacherib's army in his own day (701 B.C.) as to the defeat of the Kitti'im by the sons of light at the end of the age. In fact, the words which Peter the apostle used of the foundation-events of Christianity could equally well have been used by the

[1] See p. 88. On the relation between this historical Expounder of the Law and the Expounder of the Law who was expected to arise with the Messiah in the latter days, see p. 97.

exegetes of Qumran to express their own belief: "Moses . . . and all the prophets who have spoken, from Samuel and those who came afterwards, also proclaimed these days" (Acts 3: 22, 24).

Those who set themselves to identify the Teacher of Righteousness have been repeatedly warned to remember that the designation may have been given to more than one man—that it could, indeed, have been borne by each successive leader of the community. This may well be so; the designation could easily mean "the rightful teacher" (with a side-glance at others who gave themselves out as teachers in Israel, but had no right to do so). Even so, it seems clear that one outstanding leader, the first organizer of the community, was revered not only in his lifetime but after his death as the Teacher of Righteousness *par excellence*.

The designation, as has just been said, could easily be rendered "the rightful teacher"—or perhaps "the right guide." But it was probably derived from the Old Testament, although it would be difficult to recognize the passages from which it was taken on the basis of the English Bible alone. One of them is Hosea 10: 12, "it is the time to seek the LORD, that he may come and rain salvation upon you." The RV margin suggests "teach you righteousness" as an alternative rendering of the last clause, the point of contact between the two renderings being the fact that the Hebrew verb "to rain" is identical with the verb "to teach." This passage in Hosea could thus be understood as a promise by God to send His people a teacher of righteousness. Similarly in Joel 2: 23, "he has given you the early rain for your vindication," the AV margin suggests the variant translation, "he hath given you a teacher of righteousness."[1] The community may well have believed that these promises were fulfilled in the raising up of the great Teacher of Righteousness at an early stage in their history.

Who, then, was this Teacher of Righteousness, whose original and creative interpretation of Hebrew Scripture so influenced the thought and life of the community which revered him as its leader?

At present he cannot be identified certainly with any historical figure known to us from other sources. We can, however, piece together the fragments of information about him supplied by the texts which mention him, so as to obtain a fairly clear impression of the kind of man he was.

We have already seen that, in the belief of his followers, he had been initiated into the mysteries of the divine purpose and enabled to understand the true interpretation of the prophets of old. This is a recurring theme in the Qumran *Hymns of Thanks-*

---

[1] "Righteousness", "vindication" and "salvation" are all bound up in the Hebrew noun *sedeq* or *sedaqah*, which is used in these passages and also in the title of the Teacher.

giving, a number of which relate in the first person the experiences of one who claims to have been granted exceptional insight into the mysteries of the divine purpose.

> These things I know by understanding from thee
> For thou hast opened my ears to receive wonderful mysteries.
>
> .　　.　　.　　.　　.
>
> Thou has caused me to know thy wonderful mysteries,
> And in thy wonderful secret counsel thou hast shown forth thy power with me.

Sentiments like these find expression time and again in the *Hymns*. Of course, when the Teacher of Righteousness communicated to his followers the divine mysteries which had been revealed to him, each of them could in turn use the language of the *Hymns* to voice his own sense of privilege at being made the recipient of such wonderful knowledge. But no one could use this language so appropriately as the Teacher himself, and it is tempting to ascribe to him the authorship of many, if not all, of the *Hymns*.

What he had thus learned from God he imparted to his disciples. In a fragmentary commentary on the Book of Micah, found in Cave 1, the Teacher of Righteousness is described as "the one who teaches the law to his people and to all who offer themselves to be gathered into the elect people of God, practising the law in the council of the community, who will be saved from the day of judgment." Plainly, then, his disciples did not listen to him for instruction alone, but took practical steps to act upon his teaching, and believed that by doing so they would enjoy deliverance when the approaching judgment day arrived. In fact, the well-known words "The righteous shall live by his faith" (Hab. 2: 4) are interpreted in the Qumran commentary on Habakkuk as referring to "all the doers of the law in the house of Judah, whom God will deliver from the house of judgment [*i.e.* will justify] because of their toil and their faith in the Teacher of Righteousness." Similarly, at the end of the Zadokite *Admonition*, the promise is made that "all who hold fast to these rules, to go out and to come in according to the law, and who listen to the voice of the Teacher and make confession before God, saying, 'Verily, we have done wickedly, both we and our fathers, in walking contrary to the ordinances of the covenant; just and true are thy judgments against us'; who do not act high-handedly against His holy ordinances and righteous judgments and truthful testimonies; who learn from the former judgments wherewith the men of the community were judged; who hearken to the voice of the Teacher of Righteousness and do not repudiate the ordinances of righteousness when they hear them; they shall rejoice and be glad and their heart shall be strong, and they shall win the mastery over all the children of the world, and God shall make propitiation for them, and they shall see His salvation, for they have put their trust in His holy name."

On the other hand, those who disregarded the words of the Teacher of Righteousness were believed to have forfeited all hope of salvation.

The appearance of the Teacher of Righteousness was taken to be a sign that the closing period of the present age had set in. He was not the Messiah, but his activity meant that the messianic epoch could not be long delayed. An unspecified interval separated the "gathering in" (*i.e.* the death) of the "unique Teacher" from "the rise of a Messiah from Aaron and from Israel," according to the Zadokite *Admonition*. It has been conjectured that "Messiah" originally appeared in the plural number in this text; but in any case the Teacher played the part of a forerunner, "to make ready for the Lord a people prepared," rather than the part of a Messiah. The unspecified interval separating his "gathering in" from the rise of the messianic personage or personages referred to may have been forty years; at least we are told a few lines lower down in the *Admonition* that "from the day when the unique Teacher was gathered in until the destruction of all the men of war who returned with the man of falsehood is about forty years." The identification of "the men of war who returned with the man of falsehood" is a highly speculative matter. The expression, borrowed from Deut. 2: 14, may be figurative and need not refer to soldiers. However, their destruction was probably expected to be one of the events to take place on the very eve of the messianic appearing.

In one place in the *Zadokite Work* some interpreters have seen reference to an expectation that the Teacher of Righteousness would rise again from the dead. The passage in question is a remarkably allegorical interpretation of the "Song of the Well" in Num. 21: 17 f.—

> the well which the princes dug,
> which the nobles of the people delved,
> with the sceptre and with their staves.

The diggers are the faithful community and their activity is directed by the "Staff" *par excellence*, who is said to be the "Expounder of the Law"—that is, almost certainly, the Teacher of Righteousness.[1] Then the passage goes on:

The "nobles of the people" are those who have come to dig the well with the staves which the "Staff" established for them to walk

[1] See p. 93.

with[1] during the whole epoch of wickedness, and apart from these they will not attain their goal until there arises one who will teach righteousness in the latter days.

With this reference to "one who will teach righteousness in the latter days" we may compare the "Expounder of the Law" mentioned elsewhere[2] as destined to arise along with the Davidic Messiah at the end-time. We can scarcely doubt that the reference is to one and the same person, who is further to be identified with the anointed priest of the new age.[3] In that case the community, which acknowledged its indebtedness to the Teacher of Righteousness and Expounder of the Law whom God had raised up for it in its early days, looked forward to the latter-day appearance of another Teacher of Righteousness and Expounder of the Law. Possibly they expected him, among other things, to clear up points of legal interpretation which still remained unsolved. In other words, he would resume and bring to completion the work which the historic Teacher and Expounder had begun. But there is nothing to warrant the statement that he would be the earlier Teacher of Righteousness, risen from the dead. This may indeed have been the community's expectation, but there is no text known to us which tells us so. We know how eschatological expectations can fluctuate today among members of communities which have a strong apocalyptic outlook; this may warn us against imposing too great precision on the eschatological expectations cherished at Qumran. When the earlier Teacher arose, his followers may well have hailed him as the fulfilment of the promised "rain of righteousness" of which the prophets had spoken; but when his death left the fulfilment of all that the prophets had spoken still unrealized, they began to look for a later Teacher of Righteousness who would complete the work which the earlier Teacher had begun. So far as our evidence goes, however, the historic Teacher of Righteousness plays no messianic part in the developed eschatology of the Qumran community.

THE WICKED PRIEST

Can we say anything about the time at which the Teacher flourished? If we could identify some of his contemporaries who are alluded to in the Habakkuk commentary, we might be able to

[1] The words used are deliberately ambiguous, and could also be translated: "the laws which the lawgiver (the same word as in Gen. 49: 10; see p. 80) ordained for them to walk by".

[2] See pp. 81, 85.

[3] See pp. 87 f.

give him an approximate date; but we have to reckon with the
tantalizing vagueness with which these contemporaries are mentioned.

Of these contemporaries one is repeatedly described as the
Wicked Priest, an implacable adversary of the Teacher of Righteousness. There was one outstanding occasion on which the
Wicked Priest showed his hostility: this was when he "pursued
after the Teacher of Righteousness to his place of exile, to swallow
him up in his hot fury, and on the occasion of the appointed season
of rest, the day of atonement, he burst upon them to swallow
them up and to make them stumble on the fast-day, their sabbath
of rest." This allusion can be more easily understood when we
bear in mind that the Teacher and his followers appear to have
observed a different religious calendar from that by which the
sacred year was regulated in the temple at Jerusalem. We
gather, then, that on the occasion referred to the Teacher and
his community were observing the Great Day of Atonement in
their wilderness retreat according to their reckoning of the day,
when the Wicked Priest, for whom it was an ordinary day, invaded their meeting-place in order to throw them into confusion
and make them sin by doing acts which ought not to be done on
a "sabbath of rest."[1]

But the Wicked Priest was overtaken at last by a fearful fate,
in which the community discerned the hand of divine justice.
"Because of the evil done to the Teacher of Righteousness and
the men of his council, God gave him into the hands of his enemies,
to afflict him with a stroke, to make him waste away in bitterness
of soul, because he acted wickedly against His elect." In this
the commentator sees the fulfilment of the prophet's words:
"Will not your debtors suddenly arise, and those awake who will
make you tremble?" (Hab. 2: 7). But he gives these words a
somewhat different sense: "Will not those who bite you suddenly
arise, and will not your tormentors awake?" Then he says:
"The interpretation of this concerns the priest who rebelled and
transgressed the ordinances of God . . . therefore they smote him

---

[1] The Jewish year, according to the traditional calendar (which survives for
religious purposes to the present day), consists of twelve months which alter-
nately have thirty and twenty-nine days (corresponding to the moon's circuit
of the earth, which is completed in about twenty-nine and a half days). This
yields 354 days to a year; the approximate difference of eleven and a quarter
days required to make up the solar year is provided for by the insertion of a
thirteenth month every few years. But the Qumran community used a calendar
similar to that followed in the *Book of Jubilees*, in which the year consisted of 364
days (exactly fifty-two weeks), with twelve months of thirty days each and an
extra day added each quarter. The Sadducees and Pharisees disagreed about
certain festival datings, but they accepted the same general calendar; the Qumran covenanters differed radically from them both. In the Qumran calendar a
festival would fall in each year on the same day of the week.

with judgments of wickedness, and wrought horrors of sore diseases upon him, and vengeance upon his body of flesh."

It may be questioned, indeed, if we ought without more ado to identify "the priest who rebelled and transgressed the ordinances of God" with the man elsewhere called the Wicked Priest, but on the whole the identification seems probable enough.

The Wicked Priest had not always been so blatantly wicked as (in the eyes of our commentator and his associates) he later turned out to be. "He was called by the name of truth when first he arose, but when he ruled in Israel his heart was lifted up and he forsook God and betrayed the ordinances for the sake of wealth. He looted and piled up the wealth of the violent men who rebelled against God; and he took the wealth of nations, bringing upon himself more iniquity and guilt, and he acted in abominable ways, with every defiling impurity." This is amplified in the comment on Hab. 2: 16, 17. Verse 16 is said to refer to "the priest whose shame was greater than his glory, because he did not circumcise his heart but walked in the ways of drunkenness to quench his thirst. But the cup of God's wrath will overwhelm him, bringing more shame and ignominy upon him." The following verse (17) was apparently read thus by the commentator: "The violence done to Lebanon will overwhelm you; the destruction of the beasts will terrify you, for the blood of men and violence to the land, to a city and all who dwell therein." For this is how he explains it: "The interpretation of this saying refers to the Wicked Priest, to repay him his recompense as he recompensed the poor. For *Lebanon* is the council of the community, and *the beasts* are the simple ones of Judah, the doers of the law. God will condemn him to destruction even as he plotted to destroy the poor. And as for the words, *for the blood of a city and violence to the land*, the *city* is to be interpreted as Jerusalem, in which the Wicked Priest wrought abominable works and defiled the sanctuary of God; and *violence to the land* refers to the cities of Judah, where he plundered the wealth of the poor."

So the Wicked Priest did not even spare the poor in his greed for gain. But the commentator is thinking of a particular class of poor—his own community. For the members of the Qumran community liked to speak of themselves as "the poor," taking their cue from various Old Testament passages where "poor" and "pious" are practically synonymous. It may be, then, that one of the forms of persecution which the Teacher of Righteousness and his followers had to endure at the hands of the Wicked Priest was the confiscation of their property.

But all this ill-gotten gain would bring no good to those who laid their hands on it. The prophet had said: "Because you have plunderered many nations, all the remnant of the peoples shall plunder you" (Hab. 2: 8). And this, according to the commentator, refers to "the last priests of Jerusalem, who piled up wealth and unjust gain from the plunder of the peoples, but in the last days their wealth, with their plunder, will be given into the hand of the army of the Kitti'im, for they are *the remnant of the peoples.*"

These references to the Wicked Priest have been quoted in some detail, because they help us to come to certain conclusions about his place in history. As the Jerusalem priesthood, in any official and executive capacity, came to an end with the destruction of the temple in A.D. 70, we naturally think of him as flourishing before that date. Since he is said to have "ruled in Israel"[1] we may perhaps think of him as a member of the Hasmonean dynasty of priest-kings, who governed Judæa for some eighty years before the Roman conquest in 63 B.C.

Before we proceed, let us remind ourselves that, just as the title "Teacher of Righteousness" may have been held by more than one leader of the community, so the title "Wicked Priest" may have been given to more than one member of the priestly line in Jerusalem. Indeed, history suggests that, in general, wicked priests are much thicker on the ground than teachers of righteousness. And in the eyes of the Qumran community every ruler of the Hasmonean dynasty, not being a member of the house of Zadok, held the high-priestly office illegitimately and was *ex officio* a Wicked Priest. But, just as our texts point to one outstanding Teacher of Righteousness, they also point to one outstanding Wicked Priest, the execrated enemy of the unique Teacher.

Who then was he? One Hasmonean ruler who has special claims to be considered for the post of "Wicked Priest" is Alexander Jannaeus, who became king and high priest of the Jews in 103 B.C., and held office until 76 B.C. He was notoriously a persecutor of certain pious groups in Judæa, particularly of those who considered either his high priesthood or his ritual procedure irregular; he was, moreover, a military adventurer with an insatiable lust for conquest, and in the course of his campaigns he reduced many Gentile cities on the Palestinian seaboard and in Transjordan and added them to his kingdom, enriching himself with their plunder. When he died, his widow, Salome Alexandra, succeeded to the civil sovereignty, and their elder son, Hyrcanus II, became high priest. The years following Salome Alexandra's death in 67 B.C. were marked by civil war between the partisans

---

[1] This expression would not be decisive in itself; since the high priest was *ex officio* head of the Jewish state in post-exilic times, any high priest might be said to have "ruled in Israel".

of Hyrcanus and his ambitious younger brother, Aristobulus II;
but in 63 B.C. the Romans intervened and not only imposed peace
on the warring factions but exacted a heavy tribute from the
Jewish state. This might well be viewed as at least a beginning of
the fulfilment of the commentator's prediction that the wealth
and plunder of the last priests of Jerusalem would be given into
the hand of the army of the Kitti'im.

But the Wicked Priest is said to have been "called by the name
of truth when first he arose." How could this apply to Jannaeus?
It might possibly be a reference to his Jewish name. Jannaeus
represents Jannai, which is a shortened form of Jonathan, as we
know from Jannaeus's coinage. (Some of his coins are bilingual,
giving his name as "King Jonathan" in Hebrew and "King
Alexander" in Greek; others bear the Hebrew inscription:
"Jonathan the high priest and the commonwealth of the Jews.")
Now Jonathan was an honourable name; not only did it mean
"Gift of God," but it had noble associations in Jewish history
because it was the name of David's bosom-friend, whose self-
denying loyalty became proverbial.[1]

It might be urged against the identification of Alexander
Jannaeus with the Wicked Priest that he did not meet his death at
the hands of his enemies, and that they did not inflict torments
"upon his body of flesh." We must remember that persecuted
communities have been prone to exaggerate the torments suffered
by their persecutors, and to ascribe these to the avenging wrath
of heaven. But Alexander Jannaeus did on more than one occasion suffer crushing defeats at the hand of his enemies. In 100
B.C. he had an army annihilated and nearly lost his kingdom to the
Egyptians; in 94 B.C. another army of his was ambushed and wiped
out by Arabians in Transjordan and he escaped with his bare life;
this was followed by a revolt on the part of many of his Jewish
subjects in which he was again beaten and forced to seek refuge
in the mountains (88 B.C.). But what of the "judgments of
wickedness," the "horrors of sore diseases," the "vengeance upon
his body of flesh" with which he was smitten? The commentator
does not say (so far as we can make out) that these were tortures
inflicted upon him by human enemies into whose hands he had
fallen. But the closing years of his life were marked by a dis-
tressing bodily ailment—a quartan ague, Josephus tells us—and
when our commentator says of the Wicked Priest that "they"
smote him with judgments of wickedness and wrought horrors

[1] I owe the suggestion that "Jonathan" might be the name of truth by which
the Wicked Priest was called to E. F. Sutcliffe, *The Monks of Qumran* (1960),
pp. ix f., although Father Sutcliffe uses the argument with reference to Jonathan,
the brother of Judas Maccabaeus (see pp. 104 f.).

of sore diseases upon him, and vengeance upon his body of flesh, it is natural to infer that "they," according to a well-known Hebraic idiom, refers to the supernatural executors of divine judgment.[1] Josephus tells us, moreover, that Jannaeus's illness was the result of hard drinking; and this chimes in with the commentator's statement that the Wicked Priest "walked in the ways of drunkenness to quench his thirst."

If the struggle between the Wicked Priest and the Teacher of Righteousness is to be dated in Jannaeus's reign, it may be set in the context of other disputes which set that king at loggerheads with many of his subjects.

One story relates how at the Feast of Tabernacles, where he was officiating as high priest, he mismanaged the ceremony of the water-pouring with such deliberate disregard of what the people counted the proper ritual that the spectators pelted him with citrons (which they held in their hands as part of the requirements of the occasion). In his fury he sent soldiers among them, and a large number were slaughtered.[2]

It was in his reign that the breach between his dynasty and the Pharisees became complete; and the circumstances which so alienated the Pharisees would certainly alienate the disciples of the Teacher of Righteousness as well. Echoes of the bitterness of the conflict between Jannaeus and the Pharisees may be heard in various places throughout the rabbinical literature of later days: on several occasions reference is made in this literature to the time "when King Jannaeus put the rabbis to death."

The Talmud[3] has preserved the record of a feast in celebration of a victorious campaign in Transjordan, to which the king invited all the wise men of Israel. At this feast "there was a man, frivolous, evil-hearted and worthless, named Eleazar Ben-Po'irah," who told the king that the hearts of the Pharisees were disaffected towards him. To prove his charge, he urged the king to put on the high-priestly turban, with its plate of gold bearing the inscription: "Holy to the LORD." It was incumbent upon those who were present to rise as a token of reverence when the high priest put on this mitre. But one of the wise men present (Judah Ben-Gedidiah by name) exhorted the king to content himself with the royal crown, and leave the priestly crown to the

---

[1] A good example of this idiom appears in our Lord's parable of the rich fool (Luke 12: 16–21); the divine message to him runs literally thus: "Fool! This night *they are requiring* your soul from you . . ."

[2] This story is reconstructed by piecing together an incident narrated by Josephus in his *Antiquities* (xiii. 13. 5) and one preserved in the Babylonian Talmud, tractate *Sukkah* (48b).

[3] In the tractate *Qiddushin* (66a).

seed of Aaron. There was an implied insult in this exhortation which had already estranged Jannaeus's father, John Hyrcanus, from the Pharisees. For it was said by some that the legitimacy of John's birth was in doubt on the ground that his mother, the wife of Simon Maccabaeus, had been for some time a prisoner of war in the hands of the Seleucid authorities. They therefore doubted whether John was truly the son of Simon and consequently an inheritor of the priestly seed of Aaron. John's legitimacy, however, was vindicated after legal inquiry, but some of the sages would not be satisfied, and now the matter was raised again by way of an objection to the tenure of the high-priesthood by his son Jannaeus. The other wise men who were present at the feast appear to have preserved a discreet silence when their colleague spoke so undiplomatically. But the king asked Eleazar Ben-Po'irah what treatment they deserved, and Eleazar answered: "If you will take my advice, trample them down." Accordingly, says the Talmudic narrative, all the wise men of Israel were massacred, except Simeon Ben-Shetach (brother of Queen Salome Alexandra), who was hidden by his sister and restored the sacred law to its former glory after Jannaeus's death.

The Teacher of Righteousness and his disciples were not Pharisees. Their interpretation of the law and their discipline were severer than those of the Pharisees; indeed, they looked down upon the Pharisees as "Seekers after Smooth Things." But we may be sure that any objection which the Pharisees felt to the tenure of the high-priesthood by the Hasmoneans would be felt more keenly and expressed more vigorously by the men of Qumran. An element of legend is plainly to be seen in the Talmudic narrative, and it confuses two or three quite distinct incidents. But there is a sound historical core, and it is possible that Jannaeus's attack on the rabbis did not leave the Qumran community unscathed.

One might even toy with the idea of linking the feast given by Jannaeus to the rabbis with the occasion referred to by the Habakkuk commentator in his note on Hab. 1: 13 ("why dost thou look on faithless men, and art silent when the wicked swallows up the man more righteous than he?"). "The interpretation of this," says the commentator, "concerns the house of Absalom and the men of their council who kept silence when the Teacher of Righteousness was rebuked, and did not come to his aid against the Man of Falsehood, who rejected the law in the midst of all their congregation." Indeed, the identification of the Teacher of Righteousness with Judah Ben-Gedidiah himself has been suggested. But nothing further is known about Judah Ben-Gedidiah which could justify a more positive expression of opinion.

Who was the Man of Falsehood whom the Qumran commentator charges with rejecting the law? He could conceivably have been the Wicked Priest himself, or else someone, like Eleazar Ben-Po'irah, who aided and abetted him. But from allusions elsewhere in the Zadokite and Qumran writings it seems that he was the leader of a rival religious movement, which (in the eyes of the Teacher of Righteousness and his followers) "led the simple astray." The identification of this rival movement must be a matter for further study; it is worth considering whether the reference may not be to Simeon Ben-Shetach and the Pharisees who followed him.

As for the men of the "house of Absalom," who kept silence when they ought to have spoken out in defence of the Teacher of Righteousness, their identity remains to be determined. Some scholars have pointed out that Alexander Jannaeus had a younger brother named Absalom[1] (whose daughter married Alexander's younger son Aristobulus). But the commentator may have given the name "house of Absalom" to some group of people because he detected a resemblance between their conduct and that of Absalom, the handsome son of King David who rebelled against his father.

If we look to one of the other Hasmonean rulers to find an alternative candidate for the rôle of Wicked Priest, Jonathan, the brother of Judas Maccabaeus, invites our attention.[2] He had the same Jewish name as Alexander Jannaeus, and the statement that the Wicked Priest "was called by the name of truth when first he arose" might refer to the period between 160 and 152 B.C., when Jonathan led the forces of resistance in Judæa in succession to his brother Judas. In the latter year, however, he entered into friendly relations with Alexander Balas, pretender to the Seleucid crown, and received from him the high-priestly office. That one who was not a member of the house of Zadok should assume the high-priesthood was an offence in the eyes of the men of Qumran; but it was doubly offensive that it should be accepted as a gift from a pagan king. When, at the feast of Tabernacles in 152 B.C., Jonathan officiated in the temple in the high-priestly vestments, this might well appear to many pious Jews to be a betrayal of the holy ordinances and a pollution of the sanctuary.

[1] A. Dupont-Sommer (*The Dead Sea Scrolls*, p. 37) suggests that this Absalom may have been brother-in-law, not brother, to Jannaeus—in other words, a brother of Salome Alexandra, and therefore possibly well disposed to the Pharisees (rabbinical tradition makes the Pharisaic leader Simeon Ben-Shetach a brother of hers). But we must not use one hypothesis as the foundation for another.

[2] Among those who have identified the Wicked Priest with Jonathan may be mentioned J. T. Milik, *Ten Years of Discovery in the Wilderness of Judaea* (1959), pp. 65 ff.; E. F. Sutcliffe, *The Monks of Qumran* (1960), pp. ix ff., 42 ff.

The Wicked Priest's self-enrichment at the expense of Gentiles and of "the violent men who rebelled against God" may be illustrated by Jonathan's successful expeditions against the cities of the Mediterranean seaboard of Judæa in support of Alexander Balas, and later by the account of his sending a detachment of 3,000 soldiers to help Demetrius II to crush a revolt in Antioch, from which they "returned to Jerusalem with much spoil" (I Macc. 11: 51).

As for the Wicked Priest's disastrous end, this may be correlated with Jonathan's treacherous arrest by Trypho, acting as regent for Antiochus VI. Trypho hoped to wrest concessions from the Jews by holding Jonathan as a hostage, but when he found his blackmail ineffective, he put Jonathan to death. We are not told that Jonathan's death was preceded by torture, but this is not improbable; it would certainly agree well with the words of the Habakkuk commentator concerning the rebellious priest: "they smote him with judgments of wickedness, and wrought horrors of sore diseases upon him, and vengeance upon his body of flesh."[1]

It is further pointed out that it is precisely in the course of his account of Jonathan's career that Josephus makes his first reference to the Essenes.[2] On the other hand, our records say nothing about Jonathan's walking in the ways of drunkenness.[3] This is not conclusive, as they might have no occasion to do so.

Jonathan, then, must not be overlooked when we are endeavouring to identify the Wicked Priest, although he does not fit the bill so well as Jannaeus does.

A case has also been stated for seeing the Wicked Priest in Jonathan's brother Simon, who succeeded him as leader and high priest of the Jews.[4] But apart from the fact that Simon, as a non-Zadokite high priest, would have been *ex officio* a "Wicked Priest" in Qumran eyes, even after the high priesthood was conferred on him in 142 B.C. by resolution of the national assembly of the Jews, there is little in what we know of his character that corresponds with the descriptions of the Wicked Priest of the

---

[1] Compare the commentary on Ps. 37: 14 f., mentioned on pp. 76 f., where "the wicked" are interpreted of the enemies of the faithful priest, who are "given into the hand of the terrible ones of the Gentiles for judgment". But here the "terrible ones of the Gentiles" are more probably the Kitti'im, who in the Habakkuk commentary are the executors of divine wrath against the persecutors of the Teacher of Righteousness and his community.

[2] *Antiquities* xiii. 5. 9.

[3] J. T. Milik indeed denies that drunkenness is indicated in the relevant passage of the Habakkuk commentary, but in this denial he is in a decided minority.

[4] See F. M. Cross, *The Ancient Library of Qumran* (1958), pp. 107 ff.

Qumran commentaries. There is indeed one reference to his drinking not wisely but too well, and that is in the account of the fatal
banquet at Jericho when he was assassinated by his son-in-law
Ptolemy (135 B.C.). But that would not constitute a habitual
"walking in the ways of drunkenness to quench his thirst"; and
Simon's tragic end bears no relation to the description of bodily
torments endured by the Wicked Priest.

One argument put forward in support of Simon's identification
with the Wicked Priest depends on two premisses: (a) that Simon
is the "accursed man, one of the sons of Belial," referred to at the
end of the Testimony document from Cave 4,[1] and (b) that this
"accursed man" is the Wicked Priest. But neither of these
premisses is certain.

If the Wicked Priest is identified with one of these earlier
Hasmoneans, then another Absalom lies ready to hand to explain
the reference to "the house of Absalom" in the Habakkuk commentary—a trusted lieutenant of Judas Maccabaeus, whose sons
occupied responsible posts under Jonathan and Simon.[2]

On the whole, the identification of the Wicked Priest with
Alexander Jannaeus appears at this stage to satisfy more of the
available data than any other identification.

THE TEACHER'S IDENTITY

But even if we do tentatively identify the Wicked Priest with
Jannaeus, this does not make it much easier to put a name to the
Teacher of Righteousness, although it does provide him with a
historical setting. Some, as we have seen, have thought of Judah
Ben-Gedidiah, whose tactlessness gave such offence to Jannaeus;
others have thought of an Essene named Judah, who figures in an
incident at the Hasmonean court only a month or two before
Jannaeus's accession to the throne; it has even been supposed—
and it is nothing more than a matter of supposition—that these
two might be one and the same man. Others have thought of a
pious Jew named Onias,[3] who was stoned to death by the partisans

[1] See pp. 90 f.

[2] Cf. II Macc. 11:17; I Macc. 11:70; 14:11. But the name Absalom was
quite common, and a suitable one would probably be forthcoming in any
generation; those who date the clash between the Wicked Priest and the Teacher
of Righteousness in A.D. 66 (see p. 22, n. 3) have no difficulty in finding an
Absalom at the required place and time (Josephus, War ii. 17. 9).

[3] He was known as Onias the rain-maker because of the efficacy of his prayers
for rain. But whereas Josephus tells how he was stoned to death for refusing
to pray for rain in order to secure military advantage for Hyrcanus's forces
against those of his brother Aristobulus, the Talmud tells how he experienced
a Rip Van Winkle sleep of seventy years' duration, and died of grief soon after
he woke up because no one recognized him.

of Hyrcanus II shortly before the Roman conquest in 63 B.C. But nothing that is related of any of these good men bears much resemblance to the activities of the Teacher of Righteousness, as these can be reconstructed from the Zadokite and Qumran texts.

As the character of the Teacher has been studied with increasing interest and thoroughness during recent years, he has inevitably been compared with the Founder of Christianity. One Cambridge scholar, indeed (Dr. J. L. Teicher), has gone so far as to identify them. Others have been content with pointing out (and at times exaggerating) the features in which the Teacher appears to have anticipated Jesus. They were both founders of new communities which sprang from the commonwealth of Israel. They both laid down the outlines of a creative method of Biblical interpretation which largely served as the groundwork for their followers' theological beliefs and directed their course of action. They were both venerated by their followers; if the Qumran sect believed that the way to receive a verdict of acquittal in the divine court was to have faith in the Teacher of Righteousness, the New Testament proclaims that God justifies the man who has faith in Jesus; and in both cases Old Testament authority for this tenet was found in the words: "The just shall live by (his) faith" (Hab. 2: 4). There is this difference, however, that faith in the Teacher of Righteousness implied mainly faith in his teaching, whereas saving faith in Jesus, according to the New Testament, includes in addition personal commitment to Him as Lord and Redeemer. To His first followers Jesus was the promised Messiah; there is no evidence, on the other hand, that the Teacher of Righteousness ever claimed that dignity for himself or received it from his followers. His death, in fact, preceded the expected advent of the Messiah or Messiahs by some years; at best, therefore, he was but a precursor of the Messiah, as John the Baptist was. Indeed, he was identified with John the Baptist by the late Dr. Robert Eisler, but this identification is untenable. For (among other things) it was not at the hands of a wicked priest that John the Baptist suffered, but at the hands of Herod Antipas and his wife Herodias.

Nothing is known thus far about the manner of the Teacher's death. Attempts to show that it was a remarkable anticipation of the death of Jesus have not been successful. Professor Dupont-Sommer maintains that the horrors which were perpetrated on the Wicked Priest's "body of flesh," according to the Habakkuk commentary, were perpetrated on the Teacher, not on the Wicked Priest;[1] but this is an unnatural reading of the commentator's

[1] *The Dead Sea Scrolls*, p. 34.

language. He further holds that the passage which tells how the Wicked Priest burst upon the Teacher and his followers in their hiding-place "to swallow them up" on the Day of Atonement refers to an epiphany of the martyred Teacher which burst upon the Wicked Priest and his followers on the day of atonement in 63 B.C.—the very day which witnessed the storming of the temple area in Jerusalem by Pompey's forces.[1] But this too is a strained interpretation of the text.

Mr. J. M. Allegro, who has also taken the view that the Teacher was violently put to death, defends it by appealing to the fragmentary Nahum commentary from Cave 4.[2] He argues that, since crucifixion is mentioned in this commentary, it must have had some special significance for the Qumran community. The "raging lion" of the Nahum commentary is certainly Jannaeus, and the identification of the Wicked Priest also with Jannaeus has much to commend it. Now the Teacher of Righteousness was clearly opposed to the Wicked Priest, and since Jannaeus is known to have crucified men who rebelled against him, it is inferred that the Teacher may have suffered this fate.[3]

But there is nothing in the Nahum commentary to suggest that the Teacher was one of those who were "hung up alive." The commentary implies that those who were dealt with thus were the "Seekers after Smooth Things"; and the men whom Jannaeus is known to have crucified were men who took up arms against him and enlisted foreign aid in their rebellion. The Qumran commentator does not approve of these people, but that the "raging lion" should crucify them was to him and his associates a blasphemous outrage. This supreme barbarity might well be mentioned by a writer who wished to put Jannaeus's impiety on permanent record, without our being forced to the conclusion that the Teacher of Righteousness was one of those crucified by him.

As has been said, we simply do not know how the Teacher met his death. Nor is there any evidence that his followers attached atoning value to his death, as the early Christians did to the death of Jesus, when (following His own example) they interpreted the significance of His passion in terms of the suffering Servant of Isa. 53. The Qumran covenanters did not ignore Isa. 53, but (so far as we can tell) they did not view it as being fulfilled in

---

[1] *Op. cit.*, pp. 27 f., 44. It is, however, not at all certain that the temple was taken on the Day of Atonement.

[2] See p. 78.

[3] J. M. Allegro, *The Dead Sea Scrolls* (1956), pp. 98 ff.; "Further Light on the History of the Qumran Sect", *Journal of Biblical Literature* 75 (1956), pp. 89 ff.

the experience of the Teacher of Righteousness alone, or in that of any other individual.

When the Teacher of Righteousness died, the momentous events which his ministry was expected to usher in had not even begun to take place. Even if his followers conceived the belief that he would rise again in the latter days to continue the work which his death had interrupted, there is no evidence that he did rise from the dead, or that anyone ever thought he had done so.[1]

[1] Professor H. H. Rowley has argued for the identification of the Teacher of Righteousness with Onias III, the last legitimate high priest of the house of Zadok, who was deposed in 175 B.C. The Wicked Priest would then be Menelaus, who usurped the sacred office and procured the assassination of Onias III in 171 B.C.; the Man of Falsehood is further identified with Antiochus Epiphanes and the house of Absalom with the Jewish family of the Tobiads, whose unedifying history is recorded by Josephus. Professor Rowley's judgment is always so sound that any view which he espouses deserves the most careful consideration. His arguments are set forth in *The Zadokite Fragments and the Dead Sea Scrolls*, pp. 62 ff. A similar view is defended by the Abbé A. Michel in *Le Maître de Justice* (1954).

CHAPTER X

THE QUMRAN COMMUNITY

AN attempt can now be made to give a provisional outline of the history and character of the Qumran community. There are many gaps to be filled in, and it may be that some parts of our outline will be shown, in the light of further evidence and study, to be based on misinterpretations of the data at present available. But this is the story to which the documentary and archaeological findings seem to point.

Since the time of Alexander the Great (332 B.C.) Judæa had been under the control of Macedonian dynasties. From 312 to 198 B.C. the Ptolemaic dynasty of Egypt dominated the country; in the latter year the Ptolemies lost Judæa to the Seleucid dynasty whose capital was Antioch in Syria. But the Jews of Judæa continued to enjoy the liberal measure of home rule, under the hereditary high priests of the house of Zadok, that had been theirs under the Persian Empire. Nevertheless, the influence of Greek life and thought was very powerful, and many of the pious Jews feared that their nation's distinctive way of life, based on the law of God, would go down before the encroachments of Hellenism. They therefore banded themselves together to maintain the faith and practice of their fathers, to resist the insidious approaches of paganism, and to influence others by their example and teaching. They were known as the *hasidim*—the "pious people." Among them were some who figure in the Book of Daniel as the *maskilim*—a term which is variously translated "the wise" and "the teachers" (and it is not of great moment which of the two renderings is adopted, because those men both cultivated true wisdom themselves and taught it to their fellows).

The relative peace which the people of Judæa had enjoyed under their Hellenistic overlords began to be disturbed shortly after Antiochus IV (Epiphanes) ascended the Seleucid throne in 175 B.C. Early in his reign he interfered with the succession to the high-priesthood, and in 171 B.C. replaced the Zadokite dynasty by an upstart high priest, Menelaus, who promised to press on energetically with the policy of Hellenization in Judæa. In the following years the king was ill-advised enough to make further attacks on the Jewish way of life. At last, in 167 B.C., the distinctive features of the Jewish religion (such as circumcision and the keeping of the sabbath day) were proscribed, the sacred books of the law and the prophets were seized and destroyed, participation in pagan ceremonies was enforced throughout Judæa, and at the end of that year the temple in Jerusalem was consecrated to the worship of a pagan deity. This was the deity whose name was slightly altered by the scandalized Jews to a form which the English Bible translates as "the abomination of desolation"—or, as Dr. Moffatt rendered it, "the appalling horror."

Naturally, the pious members of the community recognized in this policy a challenge which must be resisted to the death, and great numbers of them died for their faith. In the words of Daniel, "the people who know their God shall stand firm and take action; and those among the people who are wise (the *maskilim*) shall make many understand, though they shall fall by sword and flame, by captivity and plunder, for some days" (Dan. 11 : 32, 33). But other members of the nation were not content with a passive resistance. These found leaders in an aged priest named Mattathias and his five sons (Judas Maccabaeus and his brothers), who took up arms against the oppressor and won a series of striking guerrilla victories against his forces. For a time the *hasidim* made common cause with this insurgent movement. So successful was the resistance that within three years the king and his advisers realized the folly of their action. The ban on the Jewish religion was rescinded, and exactly three years after the inauguration of the pagan cult in the Jerusalem temple, the holy place was occupied by Judas Maccabaeus and his followers, solemnly cleansed of the idolatrous pollution, and rededicated to the worship of the God of Israel.

But the situation could not simply revert to what it had been at the beginning of the reign of Antiochus IV. Judas and his men had won religious freedom by force of arms; might they not win full political independence in the same way? So they continued the struggle, and were greatly helped by increasing civil strife in the Seleucid kingdom, in the course of which one rival for the imperial throne after another tried to enlist the aid of the seasoned guerrilla force which Judas and his brothers had built up. At last, in 142 B.C., the last trace of Gentile domination was expelled from Judæa and an independent Jewish state was proclaimed, with Simon, the last survivor of the Maccabaean brothers (although he was the oldest of them), as head of the state. This meant that he was not only chief civil ruler and military leader, but high priest as well. The Hasmonean family, to which he belonged, was a priestly family indeed, but many of the *hasidim* had come to look with growing disfavour on its self-regarding ambition, and considered that its assumption of the high-priest-hood was an act of usurpation. Their relations with the Has-monean dynasty became increasingly strained in the reign of Simon's son John Hyrcanus (135–104 B.C.), and a complete breach followed soon after the accession of Alexander Jannaeus (103 B.C.). Many of the *hasidim* organized themselves as the party of the Pharisees, but one group found a leader in the Teacher of Right-eousness. Under his leadership they withdrew to the wilderness of Judæa, and organized themselves as a religious community with its headquarters at Qumran. For this withdrawal they found prophetic authority in the words of Isa. 40: 3:

> In the wilderness prepare ye the way of the LORD;
> Make straight in the desert a highway for our God.

The archaeological evidence at Khirbet Qumran suggests that the community's first settlement there (probably in the reign of John Hyrcanus) was on a modest scale; twenty to thirty years later, presumably as their numbers increased and their way of life and future policy became more clearly defined, a much more elaborate community centre was constructed.

There is a passage in the *Rule of the Community* which refers to a group of fifteen men—three priests and twelve laymen—who were to be established "in the council of the community"; with their establishment the council of the community would be well and truly founded and would be in a position to fulfil the divine purpose. It has usually been supposed that this refers to a supreme inner council which would direct the life and work of the community. But another interpretation has recently been put forward by Father E. F. Sutcliffe[1], who sees in these fifteen men the nucleus with which the Teacher of Righteousness made a beginning when he set about organizing the community.

It is likely that, in addition to the men who followed the Teacher to Qumran to live a community-life there, there were others who shared their general outlook but remained at home in the towns and villages of Judæa. It was so with the Essenes, we know; in addition to those fully initiated Essenes who lived in separated communities there were others who lived in Jerusalem and other places in Palestine. Whether the men of Qumran are to be regarded as Essenes or not, there is reason to believe that they too had their adherents and sympathizers throughout the land. While the Qumran settlement cannot have numbered more than a few hundred at any one time, their "associate members" in other parts of the country may have been ten times as numerous.

[1] *The Monks of Qumran* (1960), pp. xi, 152 f.

The Teacher of Righteousness enabled his followers to interpret the writings of the prophets in such a way as to show them the part which they had to play in the last days, which he believed were swiftly approaching. If the nation of Israel as a whole was unfit to accomplish the purpose of God, it was their privilege to act as the faithful remnant of the nation. So they were organized as a miniature Israel, comprising priests, Levites and commoners, somewhat after the pattern of their ancestors during the wilderness wanderings in the time of Moses. They bound themselves by a "new covenant" to engage in the careful study and practice of the law of God against the dawning of the new age. In fact, their faithfulness, they believed, would bring in everlasting righteousness the more speedily. They called themselves by such various titles as the *maskilim*, the saints of the Most High, the saints of the covenant, the poor of the flock, the sons of light, the men of truth, the elect of God, the sons of Zadok, the community of Israel and Aaron.

They described themselves as "volunteers for holiness"; they were men who willingly offered themselves for a highly responsible and honourable ministry. Their interpretation of the law was exceedingly strict—stricter than the Pharisaic "tradition of the elders" which incurred the criticism of Jesus in His day. They attached great importance to ritual purification by bathing in water, but they insisted that outward cleansing was useless if it was not accompanied by inward purity of heart. The cleansing which they sought, in fact, was that sprinkling with clean water, that outpouring of a new spirit, that bestowal of an obedient heart, which God promises to His people in Ezek. 36: 25 ff. They looked forward to a new Jerusalem and a new temple, where acceptable sacrifices would be offered up by a worthy priesthood. But most striking of all their beliefs is the conception of their duty as the making of expiation for their fellow-Israelites. Their devotion to the divine law, their endurance of suffering, their submission to severe discipline—all this, they hoped and believed, would be accepted by God as an atonement for the sins of the nation which had gone so far astray from the path of His will. Their duty, as they conceived it, was nothing less than the fulfilment of the rôle appointed for the obedient and suffering Servant of the Lord in Isa. 52: 13–53: 12. Did God say through the prophet: "By his knowledge shall the righteous one, my servant, make many to be accounted righteous; and he shall bear their iniquities"? Then, with God's help, they would make this their aim. And when the detailed prescriptions of their Rule were carried out "to establish a holy spirit for eternal truth, to make propitiation for the guilt of rebellion and for sinful faithlessness,

H

and to obtain favour for the land apart from the flesh of burnt-offerings and the fat of sacrifice; then [said they] the oblation of the lips according to right judgment shall be as a sweet savour of righteousness, and the perfectness of one's way as an acceptable freewill offering." It may be, too, that they looked forward to a time when one of their number would be blessed with a special endowment of the Spirit of God so as to concentrate in himself and bring to completion this cleansing and teaching ministry.

Thanks to the instruction of the Teacher of Righteousness, who had marked out the path of holiness for them and shown them how they might serve the divine purpose in the end-time, they set themselves by these means to save themselves and their less enlightened fellow-Israelites. But propitiation was not the only task which they had to undertake; when the hour struck, they would be called upon to execute the work of judgment as well. This work of judgment would be promoted by the coming war against the sons of darkness, but the guilty leaders in Israel would also reap the due reward of their deeds. For the rank and file who had been led astray there would be mercy through the community's work of propitiation; but for those who had deliberately led them astray the day of vengeance lay ahead. "By the hand of His elect God will judge all the nations; and by their rebuke those who have kept His commandments in the time of their distress will condemn all the wicked of His people."

There was no inconsistency between their propitiatory work and the execution of judgment upon the ungodly; the community was to realize not only the figure of the Servant of the Lord who makes many to be accounted righteous, but also the figure of that "one like a son of man" who, in Daniel's night vision, receives from the Ancient of Days authority to execute judgment and wield eternal and universal dominion (Dan. 7: 13 f., 22).

Their insight into the essential identity of these two prophetic figures is specially noteworthy. The two figures, as is well known, are fused in the teaching of Jesus, who derived His chosen title as Son of Man from Dan. 7: 13, but interpreted it as pointing not only to the executor of divine judgment but also to the Isaianic Servant enduring affliction for the sins of others. If He spoke of the Son of Man "sitting at the right hand of Power, and coming with the clouds of heaven" (Mark 14: 62), He also emphasized repeatedly that the Son of Man must "suffer many things and be treated with contempt" (Mark 9: 13).

It is not so generally recognized that the two figures—the Servant of the Lord and the Son of Man—were from the first *intended* to be identical; that the one whom Daniel saw in his vision was the Isaianic Servant under another guise. As close students of the visions of Daniel, as heirs of those *maskilim* whose aim (according to Dan. 12: 3) was to "turn many to righteousness," the Qumran community recognized this. Their purpose to fulfil this twofold rôle was noble indeed, even if they failed to achieve it.

When we consider the solemn responsibility to which these "sons of the covenant" dedicated themselves, we may understand why they thought it necessary to bind themselves by such a strict discipline. Only by perfect righteousness could their task of vicarious expiation be accomplished.

The true *maskil* was instructed to teach his fellows the true knowledge of God. From the emphasis on "knowledge" in several of the community documents it has been inferred by some students that the *maskilim* and their pupils pursued a form of gnosticism. That is a truism, if we understand the term *gnosis* ("knowledge") in its general sense, but it is also misleading, because by gnosticism is usually meant the pursuit of a special conception of *gnosis* which is not found in the Qumran documents. We shall look in vain here for that *gnosis* which enables the soul to liberate itself progressively from its imprisonment in matter by ascending through the spheres to the upper realm of light. The knowledge cultivated at Qumran was the knowledge recommended in the Old Testament Wisdom books, which finds its source in the fear of God. One aspect of this knowledge, however, which is specially emphasized is the knowledge of the mysteries of the divine purpose, to be unfolded in full at the end of the present world-order. One stage of this knowledge was imparted by God to His servants the prophets, but a further stage was reserved for the Teacher of Righteousness and his disciples, who were initiated into the mystery of the time when God would fulfil the things revealed to the prophets. "None of the wicked shall understand; but those who are wise (the *maskilim*) shall understand" (Dan. 12: 10). The prophets (as the apostle Peter was to say at a later date) might inquire and search diligently concerning the person or time intended by the Spirit by whose power they spoke; but these *maskilim* believed they had mastered the secret which eluded the prophets.

Another feature of gnosticism which has been detected in the Qumran writings is dualism. In the *Rule of the Community* two spirits are said to dominate human life between them—the spirit of truth and the spirit of error. "In the abode of light are the origins of truth, and in the spring of darkness are the origins of error. In the hand of the prince of lights is dominion over all the sons of righteousness, and they walk in the ways of light. And in the hand of the angel of darkness is all the dominion of the sons of error, and they walk in the ways of darkness." Certainly this may be called dualism, but it is a dualism brought into subjection to the Biblical doctrine of God the Creator, who forms light and creates darkness (Isa. 45: 7). For both these spirits are creatures of the one God, together with everything else that exists. "From the God of knowledge is everything that is and that is to be; even before they existed, He established all their design." This is emphasized more than once in words practically identical with the Fourth Evangelist's affirmation about the Divine Logos: "All things were made through him, and without him was not anything made that was made" (John 1: 3).

The organization of the community was hierarchical: there were priests (called variously "sons of Aaron" or "sons of Zadok"), Levites, elders, and the rank and file. Certain important matters were to be decided by lot, which was cast under the direction of the sons of Aaron. This preserved the tradition of earlier days in Israel when the will of God was ascertained by the priests by means of the sacred lot, the Urim and Thummim.

From time to time a general assembly of the community was held—"the session of the many," as it was called. Rules of precedence were laid down with regard to the taking of their seats —first the priests, then the elders, then the rest of the people, each in his position—and standing orders for the conduct of the meeting were strictly enforced. Anyone who wished to speak had to stand up and say: "I have a word to speak to the many." If he received permission from the leaders, he might speak. And while he was speaking no other member might interrupt him. Such unseemly behaviour as speaking foolishly, laughing out loud, sleeping while the session was in progress, or leaving the room too often without due cause, received appropriate punishment. Punishment commonly took the form of expulsion for a set period from the purificatory rites and the communal meal, or the reduction of a man's rations for a specified time.

Over each of the camps into which the community was divided there was an inspector, and over them all a chief inspector, to see that discipline was maintained.

One of the duties of this chief inspector was to examine candidates for admission to the community, to see if their motives and their lives were pure and if they understood what they were doing. Those who passed this first examination had then to appear before the general assembly of "the many" and be accepted or refused by them. If they were accepted, they had to pass through two stages of initiation, each of them lasting one year, before they were enrolled as full members. During the first year they retained their private property; during the second year it was deposited with the community treasurer, but not until one became a full member at the beginning of the third year was it merged with the common fund. A stern penalty was imposed on a member who "knowingly deceived in regard to property" —but not so stern as the judgment which overtook Ananias and Sapphira when they committed this offence in the early days of the Jerusalem church.

When a man was admitted to the covenanted community, he had to swear a solemn vow to return to the law of Moses with all his heart and shun all contact with ungodly men. While he was doing so, the priests recited blessings on those who set their hearts to walk in God's ways, and the Levites recited the curses which would descend on those who committed apostasy.

The part which marriage and family life played in the community cannot be determined with certainty. On the one hand, the *Zadokite Work* contains its own strict interpretation of the Jewish marriage law, forbidding polygamy, for example, and unions between uncles and nieces (which were not forbidden by the dominant Jewish schools of legal interpretation). The *Zadokite Work* also envisages adherents of the new covenant as living "in camps[1] according to the order of the earth" (or "land") and taking wives and begetting children; while the *Rule of the Congregation* looks forward to time when the life of the whole congregation of Israel will be properly regulated and women and children as well as men will come together to listen to the exposition of the covenant law. There is also the fact that some burials of women and children have been identified in the Qumran cemeteries. On the other hand, it is difficult to see how those who devoted themselves to the full rigours of community life at Qumran can have been able to discharge the normal obligations of marriage and fatherhood. There is no express statement in our documents that full initiation involved celibacy, and we must beware of importing into the life of the Qumran community features which we regularly associate with Christian conventual and monastic life. But, while the evidence is inconclusive, it is conceivable that those adherents of the community who lived in the towns and villages of Judæa "according to the order of the earth" married and brought up families in the usual way (following the strict Qumran interpretation of the marriage law), whereas those who lived in the wilderness as full members of the community denied themselves these comforts and responsibilities. In that case, they might be included among those referred to by

[1] The word "camps" need not invariably point to tent-encampments in the wilderness; the word is taken from the Pentateuchal law and denotes any place where people live together.

our Lord "who have made themselves eunuchs (*i.e.* have abstained from marriage and family life) for the sake of the kingdom of heaven" (Matt. 19: 12).[1]

The Qumran community attached much importance to ritual cleansing in water. This is made abundantly clear by the *Rule of the Community*, although we cannot assume that this was the purpose of the plentiful water supply and elaborate system of cisterns at Khirbet Qumran. We gather that this cleansing was not merely an initiatory rite, but one performed frequently. But it is made abundantly plain that ritual washing alone had no efficacy if a man's heart was not right with God. The washing of the body was religiously acceptable only if it was the outward sign of a purified and humble soul within. So characteristic, moreover, do these washings appear to have been that the community fellowship is commonly designated as "the purity of the many."

Communal meals, communal worship and communal consultation were regular features of the community. These communal activities, however, did not always involve the coming together of the whole community; they could be carried out wherever ten members were gathered together, provided that one of the ten was a priest. It was necessary, for example, that when they met for a communal meal, whether as a group of ten or as a larger number, the priest should say grace before they partook of bread or wine. And where there was such a group of ten, it had to be arranged that one of them was always engaged in the study and exposition of the holy law. This seems to have been arranged by relays, so that the study and exposition were carried on continuously. The night was divided into three watches, and during each watch one-third of the membership kept awake to listen to the reading and exposition, and to voice the appointed blessings.

In addition to the ordinary communal meals, there were probably special meals of a more sacred character, restricted to full members of the community. Since the *Rule of the Congregation* describes a meal in the coming age at which the Messiah of Israel would be present (although he would not be the most important person there), it is possible that the special meals at Qumran were in some sort regarded as anticipations of this future meal. But, since the Qumran community laid such stress on the priesthood and its privileges, it is even more likely that the special meals were a continuation of the weekly eating of the shewbread (or "bread

---

[1] It is possible that during Phase II of the occupation of Qumran (4 B.C.–A.D. 68) there was some relaxation of the rules which governed the preceding phase. Another fact, of doubtful relevance, is that the *Therapeutai* in Egypt, described by Philo of Alexandria (see p. 131 below), who (unlike the Qumran community) were a lay and not a priestly order, included women as well as men.

of the Presence"), which, as our Lord reminded the Pharisees, "it is not lawful for any but the priests to eat" (Mark 2: 26). The shewbread, consisting of twelve loaves which were replaced every sabbath day on the table before the invisible Presence of the God of Israel, was reserved "for Aaron and his sons, and they shall eat it in a holy place" (Lev. 24: 5–9). Moreover, when it was placed on the holy table, it was accompanied by "plates and dishes for incense" and "flagons and bowls with which to pour libations" (Ex. 25: 29); it is not unreasonable to think that what was left of the wine for libations at the end of the week was consumed by the priests at the same time as they ate the shewbread, and this may be taken along with the evidence that at the special meals the men of Qumran took wine (or must) as well as bread.

Nor is this all. The priests of Israel had as their perquisites not only the food from the table of shewbread, but also the flesh of various animal sacrifices. This last point may be relevant for the interpretation of collections of animal bones at Qumran, which were either placed in earthen vessels or buried under potsherds (the pottery in question is so broken that either account is feasible, though the former is more probable). The bones come from cattle, sheep and goats (especially goats) which had been roasted; they are evidently the relics of meals. The fact that it was considered worth while to collect these relics and dispose of them so carefully suggests that the meals of which they formed part were not ordinary meals but special ones.[1] Were they sacrificial meals? This raises the difficult problem of the practice of sacrifice at Qumran. Jerusalem was the one place where sacrifice might be offered, according to the standard interpretation of the Deuteronomic law (Deut. 12: 5–14). But if the temporary control of the Jerusalem temple by an illegitimate high-priesthood made it impossible for the men of Qumran to take part in its services, did they have an altar in the wilderness (like their ancestors in the days of Moses) on which acceptable sacrifices could be offered by their own priests?[2] Or did they content themselves with the reflection that, since normal sacrificial worship was impossible at present, the praise of pious lips was a sufficient sacrifice to God? Our evidence is quite inadequate for a definite answer to these questions; perhaps their special meals could be described as "quasi-sacrificial" (whatever meaning we may put upon that term).

[1] See F. E. Zeuner, *Palestine Exploration Quarterly* 92 (1960), pp. 28 ff.

[2] It has been suggested that the Qumran community continued to practise the purificatory rite of the "red heifer" (Num. 19) even when it had fallen into desuetude at Jerusalem: see J. Bowman, "Did the Qumran Sect burn the Red Heifer?", *Revue de Qumran* 1 (1958–59), pp. 73 ff. But the red heifer was slaughtered "outside the camp" and not sacrificed on the altar.

Those who were finally admitted as full members of the community handed over their property (as we have seen) to the common stock, which was administered by the community treasurer in accordance with the direction of the council. They appear to have done the same with the wages or other income which they acquired during their membership of the community. For it is plain that they did not shirk manual labour, and were willing to do menial service for the ungodly, showing them humble deference outwardly, while cherishing very different sentiments towards them at heart. In an important article on "The Economic Basis of the Qumran Community"[1] Professor William R. Farmer of Drew University, Madison (N.J.), points out the importance of the questions: "How could such an established community have maintained itself in so desolate an environment? How did these people subsist? How did they obtain food, clothing, writing material, cooking utensils, etc., which were necessary for their community life?" He then considers the various kinds of work that were available to them, and pays special attention to work connected with the products of the Dead Sea, work connected with the neighbouring oasis of 'Ain Feshkha, and work which might have been carried on within the community headquarters. He shows how they could have worked as agriculturalists, herdsmen, bee-keepers, potters and so forth, and could have sold various kinds of produce and manufactured articles. Nor need we suppose that all the members spent all the time at Qumran. By working in more populated parts of Judæa, and handing over to the community all their earnings apart from their bare subsistence requirements, many of them could have contributed to the maintenance of community life.

Thus, then, they pursued their chosen course of plain living and high thinking. The Roman occupation of Judæa in 63 B.C. filled them with hope that the hour of fulfilment, for which they so earnestly looked, was about to strike. But the expected signal was continually deferred. Early in the reign of Herod the Great (37-4 B.C.) they appear to have abandoned their Qumran headquarters. This could, of course, have been due to the earthquake of 31 B.C., which caused considerable damage to the building; but we may wonder why they waited for nearly thirty years before repairing the damage. Some scholars have taken the view that the community headquarters were abandoned some years before the earthquake, and have suggested various reasons for the abandonment. Here we are in the field of speculation; but there was a good deal of fighting in the neighbourhood between 40 and 37 B.C., and the situation may have been too disturbed for the

[1] In the *Theologische Zeitschrift*, July–August, 1955, pp. 295 ff.

community to stay at Qumran. Indeed, their headquarters may have suffered in the fighting, for there is clear evidence about this time of considerable damage by fire, which points rather to a deliberate attempt to burn down the place than to an accident caused by the earthquake.

Some members of the community may have remained in the area; where the majority went we cannot say. At one time it was natural to think that this was the point at which their migration to Damascus, mentioned in the *Zadokite Work*, should be placed; but fragments of the work have been found in the Qumran caves which are to be dated palaeographically half a century earlier, and it is quite likely that the references to the Damascus migration are simply an allegorical way of describing the community's withdrawal to the wilderness under the Teacher of Righteousness.

About the time of Herod's death, the community returned to Qumran. The fact that "Archelaus reigned over Judæa in place of his father Herod" did not deter them, as it did the holy family, from settling down once more in Judæa. They rebuilt Khirbet Qumran, on a more restricted scale than before, reinforced its fortifications, and continued the way of life which they had followed before their temporary exile.

But the time of the end was still delayed. Not far from their headquarters a man of priestly birth, one John the son of Zechariah (who may have been known to some of them), began to proclaim a baptism of repentance for the forgiveness of sins around A.D. 27, in preparation for the imminent advent of "The Coming One" who was to carry out a purifying work of judgment. But John's ministry does not appear to have influenced the men of Qumran. Not long afterwards another preacher in Galilee, farther north, proclaimed that the appointed time had fully come and that the kingdom of God had drawn near, and called on the people to repent and believe in this good news. But even this ministry, with its sequel on a cross at Jerusalem, caused little if any repercussion at Qumran. They continued to wait.

There were, however, other men in Israel who did not believe in waiting, but in launching an attack on the occupying power and winning the divine kingdom by force. Many of their attempts were crushed, but one which was made in A.D. 66 was attended by an astonishing degree of initial success. Many Jews thought that the Roman grip on their land was broken. What the Qumran community thought, as they saw these "men of violence" take the field against the sons of darkness, we can only guess. Even if these men were not following the detailed prescriptions of the *Rule of War*, at least they were dealing very effectively with the Kitti'im, and at the same time they showed no great love for the priestly establishment at Jerusalem. In the eyes of the Qumran community the Zealots may well have appeared to be doing the work of God and preparing the way for the new age which would follow the extermination of the Kitti'im. A well-fortified settlement like Khirbet Qumran would almost certainly have been taken over by the insurgent forces, and we need not suppose too hastily that the men of Qumran would have objected to its being commandeered in this way.

But whatever their reactions to the revolt of A.D. 66 may have been, it spelt the end of their life and their hopes in the form which they had taken since the days of the Teacher of Righteousness. For the Romans were not daunted by initial reverses. In May of A.D. 68 Vespasian, commander of the Roman forces charged with putting down the Jewish revolt, advanced upon Jericho, and took it easily (the inhabitants having fled at his approach). Since the coin record at Khirbet Qumran, so far as its occupation by the community is concerned, comes to an end in A.D. 68, it is not unreasonable to connect the violent seizure and burning of the settlement which marks the end of Phase II of its occupation with the arrival of Vespasian's forces in the region north-west of the Dead Sea.

Before the destruction of the settlement, however, the community library was stored for greater safety in the caves near the settlement. (In this a precedent had perhaps been set by the earlier generation of men of Qumran who abandoned the site temporarily a hundred years before; some have held that the cache in Cave 1, for example, was deposited on that earlier occasion.) The members of the community who survived the assault on Qumran no doubt hoped that more peaceful conditions would be restored in due course and that they would be able to return there, retrieve their books, and resume their community life. But these hopes were not to be realized. They never returned. As for their precious books, it may be that once or twice, in the course of the centuries, some people stumbled upon one or another of the caves in which they were hidden. It may even be that the recovery of some of these documents helped to bring about a reformation movement in the Judaism of the eighth century which has persisted here and there to our own day. But for the most part the books lay forgotten in the caves, slowly disintegrating with the passage of time, until their fragmentary remains were recently brought to light in such an unexpected fashion.

NOTE ON EARLIER MANUSCRIPT DISCOVERIES

It is a matter of very great interest that other manuscript discoveries in Palestine (some of them in the region with which we are specially concerned) have been reported from earlier days.

For example, somewhere about A.D. 217 the illustrious Christian scholar Origen found some Hebrew and Greek books, including a Greek version of the Old Testament Psalms (different from the Septuagint version) "in a jar near Jericho." At the time when Cave 1 at Qumran was the only one known to contain manuscripts, some people thought that Origen's jar of scrolls must have come from it; it was even incautiously suggested that a Roman lamp and cooking-pot found in the cave might have been left by him! The Greek version of the Psalms which he found was incorporated in his great critical edition of the Bible called the Hexapla.

Many centuries after Origen's time, about the year 800, we have an account of the discovery of a cave in the Dead Sea region containing manuscripts of Old Testament books and other Hebrew works. This discovery is mentioned in a letter written by Timotheus, Patriarch of the Nestorian Christians, to Sergius, Metropolitan Bishop of Elam. (Like the discovery in 1947, this one was made by accident; a Bedouin shepherd went in search of his dog, who had followed a sheep through a hole and did not come out again.)

A century or two later we have further evidence (probably relating to the discovery mentioned by Timotheus) from Qirqisani, a tenth-century writer who belonged to the Jewish sect of the Qaraites. The Qaraites, who arose in the eighth century A.D., and have survived to this day (although a great number of them perished in the Crimea during the Second World War), rejected the rabbinical traditions preserved in the Talmud and claimed to base their beliefs and practices directly on the written text of the Hebrew Bible.

Qirqisani, in an account of various Jewish sects, makes reference to one which he calls the "Cave Sect" because their literature was discovered in a cave. He quotes an earlier writer, David Ibn-Merwan, as his authority for this reference. A later writer named Al-Biruni also refers to the "Cave Sect," giving a ninth-century author as his authority. Yet another reference to the "Cave Sect" appears in the works of Shahrastani, who lived in the eleventh and twelfth centuries. According to him, this sect flourished four hundred years before the Alexandrian heresiarch Arius. As Arius was specially prominent at the time of the Council of Nicaea (A.D. 325), this indication of time (if we can place any reliance on it) points to the first century B.C. as the period of the "Cave Sect." Perhaps Qirqisani implies a similar dating for them, if there is any chronological significance in the fact that he mentions them between the Sadducees (who first appear towards the end of the second century B.C.) and the followers of Jesus of Nazareth (who arose, of course, in the first century A.D.).

It looks as if this "Cave Sect" might be identical with our Qumran community, the more so as Qirqisani tells us that it followed a different calendar from the ordinary one.

It looks, moreover, as if Qirqisani was not the only Qaraite Jew to be interested in the "Cave Sect" and its literature. There are some quite interesting points of contact between the Qumran texts and Qaraite doctrine. It is now archaeologically impossible to entertain the suggestion, made shortly after the announcement of the first Qumran discoveries, that the Qumran texts reflect Qaraite influence. But a *prima facie* case can be made out for the view that the early development of Qaraite doctrine was considerably indebted to the chance discovery of Qumran texts just about the time when the Qaraite movement originated. It is worth mentioning that it is apparently to Qaraite scribes that we owe the two fragmentary copies of the *Zadokite Work* which lay concealed for so many centuries in the Cairo genizah. Was this one of the works discovered among the literature of the "Cave Sect" in the eighth century? It seems highly probable.

CHAPTER XI

QUMRAN AND THE ESSENES

INEVITABLY we ask if there is any group of pious Jews mentioned in contemporary literature with which the community of Qumran might be identified. And, almost as inevitably, we are reminded of the people called the Essenes, concerning whom a considerable body of information is provided for us by three writers of the first century A.D. Two of these writers are Jews who wrote in Greek—the Alexandrian Philo and the Palestinian Josephus—and the other is a Roman, the elder Pliny.

Pliny's account is worth quoting in full. It comes in the fifth book of his *Natural History* and was written between A.D. 73 (the year of the reduction of Masada) and 79 (the year of Pliny's death in the eruption of Vesuvius). He has just been describing the Dead Sea and its marvels, and he continues thus:

> On its west side, just far enough from its shore to avoid its baneful influences, live the Essenes. They form a solitary community, and they inspire our admiration more than any other community in the whole world. They live without women (for they have renounced all sexual life), they live without money, and without any company save that of the palm trees. From day to day their numbers are maintained by the stream of people who seek them out and join them from far and wide. These people are driven to adopt the Essenes' way of life through weariness of ordinary life and by reason of the changes of fortune. Thus, through thousands of generations —incredible to relate—this community in which no one is ever born continues without dying; other people's weariness of life is the secret of their abiding fertility! Below their headquarters was the town of En-gedi, whose fertility and palm-groves formerly made it second only to Jerusalem; but now, like Jerusalem itself, it lies a heap of ashes. Next comes Masada, a fortress on a rock, itself also not far from the Dead Sea. And there is the frontier of Judaea.

Whoever the people may be whom Pliny is describing, his description, which is probably based on earlier sources, contains a large element of rhetorical exaggeration. For example, the Essenes had certainly not lived in that area for "thousands of generations"; ten generations would probably be a considerable exaggeration, even if we reckoned four generations to a century. Therefore perhaps we should not conclude too hastily that Pliny cannot be referring to the Qumran community, even if we can immediately spot some features of his account which cannot be reconciled with the evidence we have collected thus far about that community. As was mentioned earlier, Father de Vaux concluded, shortly after the excavations at Khirbet Qumran were begun, that here were the headquarters below which (as Pliny said) lay the town of Engedi. And yet Khirbet Qumran itself provided evidence that the community which had its centre there lived neither without money nor entirely without women, so that Pliny's statements on both these points would have to be taken with a grain of salt if Father de Vaux's identification were accepted.

Of the two Jewish writers who mention the Essenes, Philo of Alexandria was the earlier: he was born about 20 B.C. and died about A.D. 50. He has left us two accounts of the Essenes. One is a fairly long account, in his treatise *Every Good Man is Free* (which is commonly regarded as one of his more youthful productions); the other is shorter, and formed part of his *Apology for the Jews*.

In his longer account Philo estimates the numbers of the Essenes at about four thousand, and describes them as living in villages, working hard at agriculture and similar occupations, devoting much time (especially on the sabbath, when they congregated in their synagogues) to the communal study of moral and religious questions, including the interpretation of the sacred scriptures. They paid scrupulous attention to ceremonial purity, he tells us, and held all their property—money, food and clothes—in common. They abstained from animal sacrifice, from the swearing of oaths, from military service and commercial activity. They kept no slaves, made provision for those of their number who were unable to work through sickness and old age, and in general cultivated all the virtues. They were, indeed, illustrious examples of his thesis that the truly good are the truly free.

In his shorter account Philo again makes mention of several of these features, and adds that they admit none but adults to membership in their community, and that they practise celibacy, on the ground that wives and families distract men's attention from the pursuit of goodness and truth.

Josephus, who was born about A.D. 37 and lived on to the end of the century, has also given us two accounts of the Essenes. His longer and earlier account comes in the second book of his *History of the Jewish War*, which was written only a few years after A.D. 70. A shorter account appears in the eighteenth book of his *Jewish Antiquities*, written some twenty years later.

Josephus gives us more detailed information than Philo does, and his information is based—in part, at least—on first-hand

evidence. He claims, indeed, to have made trial of the Essenes
in his youth, as of the other Jewish sects, in order that, when
he had made some acquaintance with them all, he might choose
the best. Unfortunately, we can never read anything that Josephus
tells us about himself without a certain measure of reserve; and
as his "close familiarity" with the Essenes was wedged in along
with other experiences between his sixteenth and nineteenth
years it does not appear to have been very extended.

Besides, while Philo for his part admittedly uses the Essenes
to point a moral, Josephus in turn emphasizes those features in
this as in other Jewish sects which he judged would make the
greatest impression on his Gentile readers; for one thing, he
persists in describing the Jewish religious sects as schools of
philosophy after the Greek fashion.

For the most part, however, Josephus's description of the
Essenes strikes us as being factual and reliable.

According to him the Essenes were scattered through all the
cities of Palestine. Some of them lived in Jerusalem. They
practised common hospitality; an Essene from a distance would be
treated as a brother by any other Essene to whose house he came.
But much of Josephus's description implies a community life
such as could not be followed by permanent city-dwellers, and a
reasonable inference is that the fully initiated Essenes were organized in separate communities while they had attached to them
associate members who lived in cities.

In his shorter account of the sect he says:

> The doctrine of the Essenes is that all things are left in the hand
> of God. They teach the immortality of the soul, and think it their
> duty to strive for the fruits of righteousness. When they send their
> votive offerings to the temple, they do not bring sacrifices, because
> they follow exceptionally strict purificatory rules of their own; for
> this reason they are excluded from the common precinct of the temple
> and offer their sacrifices by themselves. They excel all other men in
> their manner of life, and they devote themselves wholly to agri-
> culture. A special meed of admiration should be accorded to their
> righteousness, in which they surpass all others who pursue the good
> life, without precedent among either Greeks or barbarians. Nor
> is this a temporary devotion; it has persisted among them for long
> as a settled policy. They have all things in common, so that a
> rich man enjoys no more of his wealth than a man who is penniless.
> There are more than four thousand men who follow this way of
> life, and they neither marry wives nor keep slaves, for they think
> that the possession of slaves tends to injustice, while marriage is an
> occasion of strife. But they live by themselves and serve one another.
> They appoint fit men to receive their revenues and the produce of
> the earth, and priests to supervise the preparation of their bread and

other food. They all follow the same course of life without deviation, bearing a very closer resemblance to those . . . who are called "the many".[1]

While Josephus confirms, in general, the statements of Philo and Pliny that the Essenes were celibates, he mentions one order of Essenes, "which, while at one with the rest in its mode of life, customs and regulations, differs from them in its views on marriage." Members of this particular order marry wives and bring up families, he says, because they reckon that otherwise the race would die out (a naïve explanation, since, on his showing, the major Essene groups appear to have propagated their species quite successfully by adopting and bringing up other people's children). These wives evidently shared the community life and ritual washings.

Anyone who sought admission to the Essene brotherhood, Josephus tells us, had to undergo three years' probation. During the first year he wore the white linen habit and loin-cloth which were characteristic of the sect, and carried the small trowel which every Essene used to dig a latrine-pit in accordance with the instruction of Deut. 23: 12–14. At the end of the first year the novice was admitted to the ritual purification in water, but two more years had to elapse before he was considered ready for admission to the communal meal. And when this final stage of full initiation was reached, says Josephus, "before he is allowed to touch the communal food, he is made to swear tremendous oaths: first, that he will practise piety towards God; then, that he will observe justice towards men; that he will do wrong to none whether on his own initiative or by another's orders; that he will always hate evildoers and help the just; that he will keep faith with all men and especially with those in authority (since no man achieves dominion save by the will of God); that, if he himself should be a ruler, he will not abuse his authority or outshine his subjects in dress or by any superior decoration; that he will always love truth and expose liars; that he will keep his hands free from theft and his soul pure from impious gain; that he will conceal nothing from his fellow-Essenes and reveal none of their secrets to others, even though he be tortured to death. He swears, moreover, to transmit their rules exactly as he received them, to abstain from banditry, and likewise to preserve the books of the sect and the names of the angels. By such oaths they bind securely those who join them."

As might be expected in a fellowship guarded by such oaths,

[1] The text of this last sentence is generally agreed to be corrupt, and various emendations have been suggested.

the discipline was strict; yet it was notoriously and inflexibly just. The effect of the initiatory oaths on the conscience of those who were bound by them was such that an excommunicated Essene inevitably starved to death (unless his excommunication was rescinded in time), because all food prepared otherwise than according to their rule was ceremonially unclean and he could not bring himself to eat it. Josephus tells how many members of the sect endured all kinds of tortures at the hand of the Romans, who tried by such means to force them to eat forbidden food or otherwise break their oath, but all to no effect.

An Essene's day began before sunrise, when he rose to recite morning prayers along with his fellows, "as though they were entreating the sun to rise." This probably means no more than that they said their prayers facing east, which was not the general Jewish practice.[1] Before these prayers were offered no word was spoken. Then (except on the sabbath, which was very strictly observed) the brethren betook themselves to the various tasks which were assigned to them by the overseers, and worked at them until noon was approaching. Then they assembled in the community centre, bathed, and entered the refectory in their linen habits. This midday meal was a solemn occasion at which none but full members were present. It was introduced and concluded by grace, said by a priest, and the company praised God together before and after the meal, which consisted of simple fare. They ate in moderation, and their behaviour during the meal, as at all other times, was marked by quietness and sobriety. They did not all speak at once, but spoke in turn, observing the rules of seniority. For there were four classes of members, arranged in order of seniority.

After the meal they laid aside their linen habits, resumed their working clothes, and continued at their prescribed tasks until evening. Then they assembled for another meal, but at this meal strangers and visitors might be present.

One curious feature which Josephus relates for the edification of his readers is that the Essenes regarded oil as defiling and would not anoint themselves, even after bathing, for they believed a rough skin to be more pleasing to heaven. They avoided oaths, apart from those which they swore at their initiation. They were great students of the sacred books and writings of the ancients, and had a reputation both for interpreting the prophets and for making predictions themselves, which were regularly verified by

---

[1] Alternatively it has been suggested that Josephus at this point had in mind a sect called the Sampsaeans, which probably had some affinities with the Essenes, and acquired its name (derived from the Semitic word for "sun") from acts of homage paid to the sun as a manifestation of divinity.

I

the event. They also paid much attention to the medicinal pro-
perties of various roots, plants and "stones" (probably bituminous
products of the Dead Sea).

Another writer who gives us an account of the Essenes on the
general lines of Josephus's account is the Roman Christian Hippolytus, whose treatise on *The Refutation of All Heresies* dates from
the early years of the third century. Hippolytus appears to have
had access to a reliable and independent source of information,
which enabled him to correct Josephus's account in certain points,
and to supplement it in others. Hippolytus omits the suggestion
of sun-worship in their morning prayers; according to him, "they
continue in prayer from early dawn, and do not speak a word until
they have sung a hymn of praise to God."

Hippolytus tells us that the Essenes in the course of their
history had split up into four parties, differing one from another
in several important respects. One of these parties, he says, mani-
fested such a degree of intolerance of Gentiles (especially Gentiles
who took the name of God upon their lips but refused to be cir-
cumcised) that its members were known as Zealots or *sicarii*.[1]
If this does not indicate an actual overlapping of the Essenes and
Zealots, it does at least suggest that some Essenes adopted an
attitude towards Gentiles which led people to confuse them with
Zealots. That the Essenes were not pacifists in principle seems
to be further indicated by the appearance of an Essene named
John as an energetic commander of the insurgent Jewish forces in
the war against Rome.

Hippolytus gives us a number of instances which illustrate the
strictness with which the Essenes observed the sabbath and other
laws. Some, he says, would not handle a coin which bore the
likeness of the emperor or any other man, for the very act of looking
at such a thing was regarded by them as one of the forms of
idolatry forbidden in the Second Commandment.

But his most important deviation from Josephus's account is
his statement that the Essenes believed in the resurrection of
the body, as well as in the immortality of the soul. The soul,
he says, is in their view imperishable, and rests after death in an
airy and well-lighted place, until the day of judgment arrives and
it is rejoined by the resurrected body. But Josephus tells us that
the Essenes regarded the body as the temporary and perishable
prison-house of the immortal soul, from which at death the latter
breaks free and soars on high, rejoicing at its liberation from a

[1] This was a term applied to groups of militant Jewish nationalists in the
middle years of the first century A.D. who armed themselves with concealed
daggers (Latin *sicae*) with which they despatched men whom they regarded as
traitors to the national cause.

long bondage. Both bear witness to the Essene belief in the natural immortality of the soul, which was not a characteristic doctrine of Judaism, but Josephus, not content with recording this Greek element in Essene belief, appears to have made a further concession to Greek taste by implying that the Essenes did not expect a bodily resurrection.

According to Philo, the Essenes were founded by Moses. No doubt, like the men who transmitted the main body of Jewish religious tradition, they represented their regulations and interpretations of the law as going back to Moses and bearing his authority. And when Josephus tells us that they honoured the name of their law-giver next after the name of God, and punished any blasphemous or unseemly use of his name with death, he is probably referring to Moses (although it has been suggested more recently that the law-giver in question was the Teacher of Righteousness). Again, the Essenes may be thought of as being in the spiritual succession to people like the Rechabites, who in the days of the Hebrew monarchy abjured the settled way of life in Canaan, with the cultivation of corn and wine, and set themselves to maintain the wilderness tradition of their ancestors in Moses' time. But their existence as a community cannot be traced back earlier than the middle of the second century B.C. Josephus first mentions them in his account of the governorship of Jonathan (160—143 B.C.); the first individual Essene known to history is a man called Judah, who lived in the reign of the Hasmonean king Aristobulus I (104-103 B.C.) and was renowned for his ability to predict the future.

The derivation of the name "Essene" has long been, and still is, a matter of debate. A very strong case has been made out for deriving it from an Aramaic word meaning "healer."[1] This derivation is the more interesting because it reminds us of the people whom Philo describes as *Therapeutai*—a Greek word which could mean "healers," although Philo seems to understand it to mean "servants" or "worshippers" (of God).[2] They constituted a pious body of Jews in Egypt to whom Philo points, as he points to the Essenes of Judæa, in confirmation of his thesis that "every good man is free." But we cannot trace any direct connection between them and the Essenes. Perhaps the view still most widely held about the etymology of "Essenes" is that which derives it from an Aramaic word meaning "pious" or "holy," corresponding

[1] G. Vermes, "The Etymology of 'Essenes'", *Revue de Qumran* 2 (1959-60), pp. 427 ff.

[2] The Greek verb *therapeuo* is used over forty times in the New Testament with the sense "heal" or "cure" (compare its English derivatives "therapy" and "therapeutic"); once, in Acts 17: 25, it means to "serve" or "worship" God.

in sense to the Hebrew *hasid*. There are serious difficulties in the way of accepting this derivation; but quite apart from the etymological question the Essenes do undoubtedly represent one line of development of the movement of the *hasidim*, who played a leading part (as we have seen) in resisting Antiochus Epiphanes. Another line of development may be recognized in the rise and growth of the party of the Pharisees from the latter decades of the second century B.C. onwards. But we have already suggested that the movement which found a leader in the Teacher of Righteousness also arose from the ranks of the *hasidim*.

What, then, was the relation between the Essenes and the Qumran community? Are we to make a straightforward identification of the two movements, or is there some other, fairly close, connexion between the two which falls short of outright identity?

Almost from the early days of the discoveries in Cave 1 at Qumran, an identification of the community with the Essenes has been suggested. Professor Sukenik was one of the first to do so. Father de Vaux identified Khirbet Qumran with the Essene headquarters mentioned by Pliny. Professor Dupont-Sommer has popularized the idea in three books, translated into English under the titles *The Dead Sea Scrolls* (1952), *The Jewish Sect of Qumran and the Essenes* (1954), and, most recently, *Essene Writings from Qumran* (1961); so also has J. M. Allegro in *The People of the Scrolls* (1959). And several other writers have favoured the view that the Qumran community was an Essene group.

What are the arguments in favour of the identification?

We have noted the geographical argument in favour of identifying Khirbet Qumran with the Essene headquarters below which, according to Pliny, the town of En-gedi lay. This argument depends on our taking "below" to mean not lower in relation to sea-level, but farther south, as on a map of normal orientation. In addition, we are assured by those who know the region that there are no other ruins in the area which could be identified with the headquarters referred to by Pliny.

Then there is a chronological argument: the Essenes are known to have flourished during the time when the Qumran community was in being—they make their appearance in history about the same time as the beginning of the Qumran movement, in the second half of the second century B.C., and were still flourishing in the second half of the first century A.D.

More important is the argument based on the similarity between the beliefs and practices of the Essenes, as contemporary writers describe them, and those of the Qumran community, as attested in their own literature.

There are striking similarities (which do not, however, amount to complete identity) between the two in respect of the long period of probation, the solemn oaths sworn on initiation, the strict discipline, the baptismal washings, the common meal, the hierarchical organization with exact observance of the rules of precedence, the place of honour and responsibility given to priests, the community of goods, the rigorous interpretation of the sabbath law and the pursuit of an unusally high and exacting standard of righteousness. Since the *Rule of the Community* makes it clear that a common penalty at Qumran was the reduction of rations, we can easily understand how a member whose offence was so serious as to warrant complete withdrawal of rations for a sufficiently long time could be in danger of death by starvation, as Josephus tells us. Sometimes the similarity between the two disciplinary codes extends to matters which we should regard as trivial; thus Josephus's statement that the Essenes avoided spitting "into the midst" or to the right is paralleled by the regulation in the *Rule of the Community* that a man who "spits into the midst of the session of the many" shall be punished—by suspension from a share in the communal meal?—for thirty days.

From Josephus's statement that "if ten are in session together, no one of them will speak if the other nine are against it" we might reasonably infer that ten was a normal grouping of their membership, and this reminds us that at Qumran ten might engage in the regular communal activities provided that the ten included a priest. But since ten was a recognized number for communal activity among the Jews in general (to this day it is the quorum necessary for a synagogue congregation among orthodox Jews), no weight can be put on this coincidence.

Josephus's testimony to the Essenes' intensive study of the ancient scriptures, particularly the prophetic writings, may find ample illustration in the Qumran texts. On the other hand, the instances he gives of the Essenes' gift of prophecy appear trivial in comparison with the forecasts of coming events, based on the interpretation of Old Testament prophecy, which we find in the Qumran texts. His reference to the Essene interest in angels is in keeping with the attention which was paid at Qumran to late Jewish works in which angels figure prominently.

Hippolytus tells us that the Essenes expected a universal conflagration at the time of the last judgment; this belief finds expression in the Qumran *Hymns of Thanksgiving*, in terms which suggest Zoroastrian influence:

The foundations of the mountains are burned up;
The roots of flint become torrents of pitch:

It devours even to the great abyss;
The torrents of Belial break forth into Abaddon.

But, in spite of all the similarities and parallels that can be adduced, we cannot feel too happy about an outright identification of the Qumran community with the Essenes. Where prominent features of the one body are not related at all in the sources of our information about the other, we cannot reach indisputable conclusions. Again, both bodies no doubt modified their beliefs and practices to some extent in the course of the years, so that we should not lay too much emphasis, perhaps, on divergencies between the Essenes and Qumran with regard to the frequency and significance of baptismal lustration, the years during which a man's probation lasted, sacrificial doctrine and procedure, the attitude towards the government (Jewish or Gentile) and the use of force. Yet there are so many hints in ancient writings of a bewildering variety of messianic and baptist groups with their headquarters in the Jordan valley and Dead Sea region that we should be cautious before we make a complete identification of two of these groups concerning which we are now better informed than we are about the others.

There is the possibility that the Qumran community should be identified with the marrying Essenes of whom Josephus speaks. Those marrying Essenes were plainly very exceptional Essenes, for not only Pliny and Philo but Josephus himself record celibacy as one of the characteristic features of Essenes in general. There is no evidence that the men of Qumran were celibate on principle, although, as we have seen, there are practical considerations which make it not unlikely that those of them who were fully initiated did abstain from marriage and family life. Another possibility is that Josephus's marrying Essenes were those associate members of the brotherhood who did not withdraw from the ordinary ways of life in the world.

The Essenes are mentioned only in Greek and Latin documents. It may be asked whether the Qumran community can be identified with any group mentioned in Jewish rabbinical literature, which is written in Hebrew and Aramaic. Here too we are unable thus far to say anything certain. We may think of those people known to rabbinical tradition as the "morning bathers" because they indulged in a ritual washing at dawn before they took the name of God upon their lips—thus exceeding the righteousness of the Pharisees, with whom they entered into controversy. But in view of the variety of baptist sects in the Judaism of those days, a verdict of "Not Proven" is all that our present knowledge warrants.

It seems clear that the term "Essenes" was a comprehensive one. Hippolytus distinguishes four parties of Essenes which differed from one another in a number of important respects, and there may have been other groups which were loosely designated by the same name. When we consider the resemblances between the known features of the Qumran community and what we are told of the Essenes, and consider on the other hand the differences between them, a reasonable conclusion is that the Qumran community was one Essene group, diverging in several particulars from other Essene groups.

But if this conclusion can be upheld, an important consequence follows. We have now for the first time a large body of Essene literature, which must henceforth be regarded as our primary source for knowledge about the Essenes, taking precedence over other ancient accounts of them, which were all written by non-Essenes.

CHAPTER XII

QUMRAN AND CHRISTIANITY

WHAT happened to the Qumran community after the destruction of their headquarters in A.D. 68? Neither the archaeological evidence on the site nor the contents of their library can in the nature of the case give us a direct answer to this question. But it need not remain completely unanswered.

It may be that the torments which Josephus describes as inflicted by Romans on members of the Essene sect, to force them to violate their solemn oaths, were endured by some of the fugitives from Qumran, as well as by members of similar groups. But some at least would escape with their lives. Their beliefs and expectations would inevitably undergo considerable modification by reason of the events of A.D. 70, but they would not be changed beyond recognition. And there is some evidence that certain beliefs and practices akin to those maintained at Qumran reappeared in other communities, possibly under the influence of men of Qumran who escaped the destruction.

Professor Oscar Cullmann, for example, has pointed out that we may have to reconsider the whole question of the origin of the Mandaeans, a fascinating Mesopotamian sect of Palestinian origin, gnostic belief and baptist practice, in the light of the new evidence from Qumran. This is certainly a matter for re-examination. But there is another sect whose beliefs and practices call for fresh study in the light of the new discoveries. This is the Ebionite sect, consisting of Jewish Christians who deviated considerably not only from the main stream of Catholic Christianity but also from the Christianity enshrined in the New Testament, even in its earliest and most Jewish stages.[1] There is now some reason to suppose that several of these Ebionite deviations, in doctrine and procedure, were introduced under the influence of men from Qumran in the years following A.D. 70.

We are told by Eusebius that, before the siege of Jerusalem began, the disciples of Jesus in that city, believing in its impending doom, fled to Pella, east of the Jordan. And it is in the region east of the Jordan that the Ebionites appear to have been strongest in the following generations. It would not really be surprising

---

[1] Cf. *The Spreading Flame*, pp. 279 ff. The fact that the Qumran covenanters, like these Jewish Christians, called themselves *'ebyonim* (i.e. the "poor") is one of Dr. Teicher's arguments for identifying the two groups.

if they were joined there by others who fled from the Roman vengeance. That these others may have included refugees from Qumran is rendered the more probable by striking affinities in thought and practice which have been detected by a comparison of parts of the later Ebionite literature with the literature of Qumran. It would be going too far to say that Ebionitism represents an amalgamation of primitive Jewish Christianity and the sytem of Qumran, for Ebionitism remained fundamentally Christian; but the particular emphasis and direction which made Ebionite Christianity so distinctive can be explained rather convincingly in terms of its incorporation of remnants from Qumran. Two European scholars who have paid special attention to this fascinating possibility are Professor Cullmann[1] and Professor H. J. Schoeps,[2] both of whom had established their reputations as authorities in the Ebionite field before the Dead Sea Scrolls came to light.

But, no matter how interesting this question is, there is another more interesting by far. Did the Qumran community have any influence on Christianity, or at least some contact with it, *before* the dispersal of A.D. 68? If (as seems probable) the Qumran community was established before the birth of Christ, was Christianity in any way indebted to it? And, more generally, do the Qumran discoveries give us fresh help in understanding the New Testament?

When the discovery of the scrolls was first announced, it was believed by many that their chief importance would lie in the new light which they could throw on the history of the Old Testament text. And, as has been indicated in an earlier chapter, the light which they throw on this field of study is of high value. But with the emergence and examination of so many more documents from the neighbourhood, and the excavation of Khirbet Qumran, the emphasis has changed more and more from the Old Testament to the New Testament side. An odd rumour went around some years ago to the effect that New Testament scholars were boycotting the study of the Qumran texts, presumably for fear that they might throw unwelcome light on the origins of Christianity. Nothing could be farther from the truth. As soon as it became evident that the study of these texts was highly

[1] A particularly powerful argument for the incorporation of the remnants of the Qumran movement in this stream of Jewish Christianity is given by Professor Cullmann in his essay "Die neuentdeckten Qumran-Texte und das Judenchristentum der Pseudoklementinen," contributed to the volume of *Neutestamentliche Studien* presented to Rudolf Bultmann (1954), pp. 35 ff. *Cf.* also his article on "The Significance of the Qumran Texts for Research into the Beginnings of Christianity" in *The Scrolls and the New Testament*, ed. K. Stendahl (1958), pp. 18 ff.

[2] *Cf.* his *Urgemeinde, Judenchristentum, Gnosis* (1956), pp. 69 ff.

relevant to the study of the New Testament and of Christian origins, they received the closest attention from New Testament scholars, and still continue to do so. It is instructive to look through back numbers of two journals for New Testament study founded in recent years—*New Testament Studies* (Cambridge, founded in 1954) and *Novum Testamentum* (Leiden, founded in 1956)—and see how many contributions to them deal with the relation between Qumran studies and the New Testament. It is equally instructive to look through the successive numbers of the even more recent *Revue de Qumran* (Paris, founded in 1958) and see how many contributions to this journal, which exists for the promotion of Qumran studies, come from New Testament scholars. Some of the earliest important studies in the Qumran field by New Testament scholars, from 1950 onwards, were collected in a volume entitled *The Scrolls and the New Testament*, edited by Professor Krister Stendahl of Harvard and published in 1958. In August 1960 the international *Studiorum Novi Testamenti Societas* devoted practically the whole of its annual meeting to the bearing of the Qumran literature on New Testament studies.[1]

Opinions differ widely on the bearing which the Qumran discoveries may have on the rise and early progress of Christianity. And the reason of this wide difference of opinion is quite simple. It is that, among the documents published to date, no unambiguous evidence has come to light which affords an explicit contact with Christian origins. We need not take too seriously the judgment which (as reported in the British press) appeared at the beginning of 1958 in *Komsomolskaya Pravda*, the organ of the Russian Communist youth movement, that the Qumran discoveries conclusively prove that Jesus never existed. (Fortunately, more objective Qumran studies than this one have been published in Russia.) But when we consider the varying judgments of those who have undertaken serious study of the Qumran texts, we must realize that very much depends on divergences of individual interpretation, and even, it may be, of presupposition on the part of those who have undertaken their study. So, on the one hand, Father Kevin Smyth, an Irish Jesuit scholar, says that to

---

[1] One of my earliest incursions into the Qumran field was the reading of a paper on "Qumran and Early Christianity" at the 1955 meeting of the *Studiorum Novi Testamenti Societas* (later published in *New Testament Studies* 2 [1955–6], pp. 176 ff.). It was not the only paper on a Qumran subject read at that meeting; indeed, on that occasion no subject aroused more animated discussion than the implications of Qumran for New Testament study. It was therefore with special interest that, a few weeks later, I read in a popular work on the subject that "New Testament scholars, it seems, have almost without exception boycotted the whole subject of the scrolls" (Edmund Wilson, *The Scrolls from the Dead Sea*, p. 131). Even when these words were written they were demonstrably fallacious.

compare the scrolls with the New Testament without taking into account the wealth of relevant information from the later Old Testament, apocryphal, pseudepigraphic and rabbinical literature, "is like comparing a fish and a man because both are wet after coming out of the sea." Against those who have seen in Qumran the soil from which Christianity sprang, he says: "Rather, it was from soil such as this that sprang the thorns which tried to choke the seed of the Gospel."[1]

On the other hand, we have Dr. J. L. Teicher maintaining that the Teacher of Righteousness was none other than Jesus, while the Qumran community consisted of Jewish Christians of the kind commonly known as Ebionites. Dr. Teicher's arguments, which were published mainly in several issues of the *Journal of Jewish Studies* between 1950 and 1955, have not convinced other scholars, although he has commented on the paradoxical situation that he, a Jewish scholar, finds himself defending the originality of Jesus against some Christian scholars who have found in the Teacher of Righteousness one who anticipated the teaching, passion and messianic claims of Jesus and have seen in the Qumran community an adumbration of the primitive Christian Church.

Among the scholars who have taken this latter line are Professor Dupont-Sommer and Mr. J. M. Allegro. We have mentioned some of their arguments in the chapter on "The Teacher of Righteousness." Professor Dupont-Sommer concluded that "the Galilæan Teacher, as he is presented to us in the New Testament writings, appears in many respects as an astonishing reincarnation of the Teacher of Righteousness."[2] Mr. Allegro says that the expectations of the early Church with regard to the Second Coming of Christ "are extraordinarily like those of the sect about their own Teacher, persecuted and crucified, and expected to rise again as priestly Messiah." He adds: "It now seems probable that the Church took over the sect's way of life, their discipline, much of their doctrine, and certainly a good deal of their phraseology, in which it is now seen that the New Testament abounds."[3]

It is such views as these that were popularized by Mr. Edmund Wilson in his book *The Scrolls from the Dead Sea* (1955); on the strength of them he hazards the suggestion that Khirbet Qumran "is perhaps, more than Bethlehem or Nazareth, the cradle of Christianity" (p. 129). And it was on the strength of such views, doubtless, that a distinguished archaeologist wrote in the course of an article on Khirbet Qumran in the *Illustrated London News*

---

[1] *The Irish Digest*, June, 1956, pp. 31–34 (condensed from *Studies*).

[2] *Aperçus préliminaires sur les Manuscrits de la Mer Morte* (1950), p. 121. Cf. the English translation, *The Dead Sea Scrolls* (1952), p. 99.

[3] *The Radio Times*, January 13, 1956, p. 9. See p. 108 above.

of September 3, 1955: "John the Baptist was almost certainly an Essene, and must have studied and worked in this building; he undoubtedly derived the idea of ritual immersion, or baptism, from them. Many authorities consider that Christ Himself also studied with them for some time. If that be so, then we have in this little building something unique indeed, for alone of all the ancient remains in Jordan, this has remained unchanged—indeed, unseen and unknown, to this day. These, then, are the very walls He looked upon, the corridors and rooms through which He wandered and in which He sat . . ." These are no more than theories, although the theory of John the Baptist's association with Qumran is less improbable than that of our Lord's residence there. But when a well-known archaeological authority states these theories in such unqualified terms, the ordinary reader may reasonably suppose that there is some archaeological evidence for them, and thus far there is none.

In so far as theories of this kind are based on the supposition that the Teacher of Righteousness claimed to be a Messiah, or that his followers believed him to be one, they have been dealt with already in this book; and it may suffice to repeat here that there is no evidence that the Teacher ever made such claims for himself, or that his followers ever thought of him as a messianic figure. We do not know the circumstances in which he died— or "was gathered in," to use the Qumran phraseology. Nor is it suggested in the published texts that his followers attached any saving significance to his death. If they believed that he would be raised again in advance of the more general resurrection for which Dan. 12: 2 taught them to look, they may have envisaged his resurrection ministry in a way corresponding to the expectation which many of their fellow-Jews cherished with regard to the prophet Elijah. Elijah, it was widely believed (on the basis of Mal. 4: 5 f.), would one day return to earth from that realm to which he had been snatched away in a whirlwind so many centuries before; and his return would be a signal of the near approach of "the great and terrible day of the LORD," for which his new ministry would prepare the people. Jesus taught His disciples to recognize the fulfilment of this expectation in the ministry of John the Baptist, His own precursor. But there is nothing to suggest that the men of Qumran regarded their Teacher, even in resurrection, as a reincarnation of Elijah. Neither is there any convincing evidence that they thought that the Teacher of Righteousness or Expounder of the Law whom they expected to arise in the end-time with the princely Messiah would be their former Teacher risen from the dead. It seems much more probable that the historic Teacher of Righteousness was in their eyes a messianic forerunner, but not a messianic personage himself.

Professor Cullmann thus goes too far when he suggests that just such a figure as the Teacher of Righteousness is envisaged in the words which Jesus speaks in the rôle of the Good Shepherd in John 10: 8: "All who came before me are thieves and robbers."[1] Had the Teacher made messianic claims for himself, he would no doubt have been included in this condemnation; but certainly neither Jesus nor the Evangelist wished to characterize the prophets and righteous men of earlier days as "thieves and robbers." In fact, we may agree that the Teacher was indeed a preparer of the way for the Messiah, although not in a sense which either he or his disciples would have recognized at the time.

Those who deny or doubt the messianic character of the Teacher of Righteousness are not necessarily moved by prejudice or an excessive preference for their accepted traditions; their concern is rather that at this stage in the inquiry students should not run too far in advance of the documentary evidence. But on the other hand those scholars who, like Professor Dupont-Sommer, draw inferences which their colleagues believe to be unwarranted should not have unworthy motives ascribed to them, as though (for example) they were over-anxious to deny the originality of Jesus and the element of divine revelation in Christianity. Scholars may disagree violently with one another's interpretations, and engage vigorously in debate; far more progress will be achieved in this way than by a mute agreement to differ. But when suspicion is thrown upon their intellectual integrity or the purity of their motives, a barrier is placed in the way of that fertile intercourse of minds to which the advancement of knowledge owes so much.

The wilderness of Judæa, in which the covenanters of Qumran established their place of retreat, figures in the Gospel narrative now and then. It was there (according to Matt. 3: 1) that John the Baptist began his public preaching; it was there that Jesus spent the forty days of temptation (Matt. 4: 1); it was there, too, that Jesus spent a few quiet days with His disciples before His last visit to Jerusalem (John 11: 54). But the wilderness of Judæa was a much wider area than the immediate vicinity of Qumran, and it was possible to spend quite a long time in the wilderness without ever coming into touch with the Qumran community.

Still, some possibilities are more probable than others. And little can be urged, in terms of probability, against the possibility that John the Baptist at one stage of his career had some contact with the Qumran covenanters or with some other people very like them. At the end of Luke's account of the birth and infancy

[1] *The Scrolls and the New Testament*, p. 31.

of John, he says that "the child grew and became strong in spirit, and he was in the wilderness till the day of his manifestation to Israel" (Luke 1: 80). The implication of these words is that, for a number of years preceding the start of his baptismal ministry, John resided in the wilderness of Judæa. Now, if a congenial retreat was found there by a youth who was born in a city of Judæa and was later to be active in the Jordan valley, it would not have been far from the neighbourhood of Qumran. And one who was of priestly birth, as John was, might have found something specially appealing in a movement which attached such importance to the preservation of a pure priesthood.

A further contact between John and Qumran might be looked for in their baptismal teaching and practice. But it is a curious fact that Josephus's account of John's baptismal teaching accords more closely with the Qumran doctrine than does the New Testament account. When we read in the *Rule of the Community* that the man who is impure and rebellious in heart cannot hope to be cleansed by ritual washing in water, we are reminded of Josephus's statement that John "taught that baptism would be regarded as acceptable by God provided that they underwent it not to procure pardon for certain sins but with a view to the purification of the body when once the soul had been purified by righteousness." Josephus's statement differs, in emphasis at least, from the New Testament description of John's baptism as "a baptism of repentance for the remission of sins." It may well be that Josephus, who was not born until some eight years after John's death, interpreted his baptismal activity in terms of a baptismal doctrine with which he himself was more familiar—the doctrine of the Essenes. But if that is so, it would follow that John's baptismal doctrine represented a deviation—perhaps a deliberate one—from that of the Qumran covenanters and other Essenes.

John was an ascetic; he came, we are told, "eating no bread and drinking no wine" (Luke 7: 33). The Qumran covenanters were ascetics too, but not to that extent. Their food was simple, to be sure, and they ate in moderation, but they did not restrict themselves to locusts and wild honey, as John did. (Of course, if one were writing historical fiction, it would be possible to explain that John had been excommunicated from the group and, in view of his stringent vows taken at initiation, was prevented from eating any other kind of food!) John proclaimed the urgent necessity of repentance, because "The Coming One" was about to execute a purifying judgment with wind and fire. The Qumran covenanters also thought in terms of an imminent judgment, but they were not the only people who did so, and they did not issue a public call to national repentance, as John did.

John may have had some contact with the Qumran community; he may even have belonged to it for a time. There is no real evidence of this at present, but if some evidence to this effect came to light, it would be welcomed by a number of students as confirmation of something which they had already surmised. One South African scholar,[1] indeed, finds hints in the first two chapters of St. Luke's Gospel that the statement already quoted ("the child grew and became strong in spirit, and he was in the wilderness until the day of his manifestation to Israel") represents a compression of a fuller account. According to this fuller account, he thinks, John's parents (who were both well on in years when he was born) died while he was still quite young, and he was adopted and brought up by the Essenes of Qumran. This may have been so. But in the present state of our certain knowledge, such a reconstruction belongs more to the realm of historical fiction than to that of real history.

But even if John did owe some debt to the Qumran community, or to any other Essene group, the ministry by which John made his mark cannot be brought within an Essene framework. He describes himself as a voice crying to Israel:

In the wilderness prepare ye the way of the LORD;
Make straight in the desert a highway for our God.

These words of Isa. 40: 3 had already been invoked by the Qumran covenanters as divine authority for their withdrawal to the wilderness. But John used them in a new sense. The divine intervention foretold by the prophet, of which the return of the exiles in the time of Cyrus was but a preliminary earnest, was about to be fulfilled. And it was a new impulse which sent John forth "to make ready for the Lord a people prepared" (Luke 1: 17). His recorded ministry is distinctively and essentially a prophetic ministry. And when "the word of God came to John the son of Zechariah in the wilderness" (Luke 3: 2), as it had come to many a prophet before, he learned and proclaimed the necessity of something more than the teaching or action of Qumran. If he had previously been associated with that community or a similar one, it was now time to break with them and follow a new path, marked out for him by God. The multitudes that flocked to the Jordan valley to hear him did so because they recognized in his preaching a note of authority the like of which had not been heard

[1] A. S. Geyser, "The Youth of John the Baptist," *Novum Testamentum* 1 (1956), pp. 70 ff. Cf. J. A. T. Robinson, "The Baptism of John and the Qumran Community", *Harvard Theological Review* 50 (1957), pp. 175 ff.; W. H. Brownlee, "John the Baptist in the New Light of Ancient Scrolls," in *The Scrolls and the New Testament*, ed. K. Stendahl (1958), pp. 33 ff.

in Israel for many a long day; "all held that John was a real prophet" (Mark 11: 32). It is not as a disciple of the Teacher of Righteousness, but as a new teacher of righteousness who had his own following of disciples, that we know the historical John the Baptist.

If the present state of our knowledge does not permit us to speak more positively about the possible contact between John the Baptist and Qumran, what can be said about Jesus Himself in this regard? John at least was an ascetic; but Jesus, on His own testimony, was not. To those who found fault with John's ministry and His own alike, He said: "John the Baptist has come eating no bread and drinking no wine; and you say, 'He has a demon.' The Son of man has come eating and drinking; and you say, 'Behold, a glutton and a drunkard, a friend of tax collectors and sinners!'" There is no flavour of Qumran about His way of life. Again, John at least is known to have lived in the wilderness before he began his public ministry; so far as we know, Jesus lived in Galilee continuously from His childhood to His baptism, apart from an occasional festival visit to Jerusalem. It was from Nazareth that He came to be baptized by John, and only after that did He retire to the wilderness of Judæa. The forty days that He spent there fasting would not afford much opportunity of initiation into the wisdom of Qumran, if indeed He spent them anywhere in that vicinity. (The traditional site of the temptation is some twelve miles north-west of Qumran.) If, in the course of His wilderness temptations, He was tempted (as seems certain) to achieve His messianic destiny by other paths than that of the Suffering Servant, marked out for Him at His baptism, then among those other paths which He repudiated the way of Qumran, in many of its aspects, must be included.

It is easy to go through the recorded teaching of Jesus and list parallels—some of them quite impressive—with what we find in the Qumran texts. This sort of thing has been done already in relation to the Gospels and rabbinic literature. It has long been known that some kind of parallel can be found in the Talmud to practically every element in the ethical teaching of Jesus. It is idle to feel alarm at this, as though the originality of Jesus and the divine authority of Christianity were imperilled by such a recognition. For He accepted the same Biblical revelation as did the Qumran covenanters and the rabbis in the main stream of Jewish tradition, and it would be surprising if no affinity at all were found between their respective interpretations of that revelation, on which their respective teachings were based.

It has often been pointed out, for example, that in His interpretation of the Old Testament marriage law our Lord approximated to the Pharisaic school of Shammai rather than to that of Hillel—surprisingly, some have felt, because in general the Pharisaism which He condemned was that of the school of Shammai. Even so, there was an important difference between His attitude and that of both Pharisaic schools. For Shammai and Hillel's difference in this regard arose from their divergent interpretations of the legal prescription of Deut. 24: 1–4, where divorce is permitted for "some unseemly thing" in the wife. The two schools disagreed on the definition of "some unseemly thing." But our Lord dismissed this legal prescription as a temporary concession made because of men's hardness of heart, and insisted that the marriage law should be interpreted in the light of the original purpose of the institution: "From the beginning of creation, 'God made them male and female' . . . What therefore God has joined together, let not man put asunder" (Mark 10: 6–9). To these words we find a closer verbal similarity in one of the Qumran texts than we find in any of our rabbinical sources. In a passage in the Zadokite *Admonition* certain people are condemned "for taking two wives in their lifetime, although the basic principle of creation is 'He created them male and female,' and those that went into the ark 'went into the ark two by two.'" Here the appeal to the Creator's institution of marriage is found, as in the teaching of Jesus. But the resemblance may be mainly verbal. It is polygamy rather than divorce that the *Admonition* condemns (divorce under certain conditions is permitted in the Zadokite *Laws*); and what the author of the *Admonition* is really attacking is the teaching of those rabbis who permitted polygamy. To him (as we have seen) polygamy is a form of fornication, and so is another practice which was condoned by the same rabbis—marriage between uncles and nieces.

When we come to the interpretation of the sabbath law (which first led to an open cleavage between Jesus and the rabbis of His day), we do not find even a verbal similarity between the Gospels and the Qumran texts. In the Gospels it is taken for granted that even the strictest rabbis would allow a domestic animal to be rescued if it fell into a pit or cistern on the sabbath day. But the sabbath regulations in the Zadokite *Laws* are more stringent. A human being may be rescued under such conditions, but not an animal. "Let no one assist a beast in birth on the sabbath day. Even if she drops her new-born young into a cistern or pit, let him not lift it up on the sabbath." About twenty-five sabbath regulations are listed among the Zadokite *Laws*, and they are totally incompatible with the attitude expressed in Jesus' words: "The sabbath was made for man, not man for the sabbath" (Mark 2: 27). For Jesus' interpretation of the sabbath law, as of the law of marriage, was based on the purpose for which the sabbath was originally instituted.

One very interesting point of contact between the Qumran texts and the New Testament has been emphasized by a number of scholars recently, notably by Professor W. F. Albright in his Pelican book *The Archaeology of Palestine* and in a paper on "Recent Discoveries in Palestine and the Gospel of St. John" which he contributed to *The Background of the New Testament and its Eschatology* (a volume of essays published in 1956 in honour of Professor C. H. Dodd). This point of contact is found in a comparison of the distinctive vocabulary of the Fourth Gospel with that of some of the Qumran documents.[1] Such characteristic Johannine expressions as "the sons of light," "the light of life," "walking in darkness," "doing the truth," "the works of God," turn up in the writings of the Qumran community. Like the Qumran community, John sees the universe in terms of sharply contrasted light and darkness, good and evil, truth and falsehood. If Professor Albright's conclusion is valid, that John (and other New Testament writers as well) "draw from a common reservoir of terminology and ideas which were well known to the Essenes and presumably familiar also to other Jewish sects of the period," scholars may be less inclined to trace these features to Hellenistic sources. Some may bethink themselves at this stage of the high probability that the Beloved Disciple was a follower of John the Baptist before he was called by Jesus. But the affinities in vocabulary should not make us overlook the new element in John's use of these terms. When he speaks of the true light, he is not thinking in abstractions; he is not primarily concerned with a body of teaching or a holy community; to him the true light is identical with Jesus Christ, the Word made flesh. And Professor Albright wisely emphasizes the "wide gulf between the doctrines of the Essenes and the essentials of Johannine teaching." He lists four essentials of the teaching of John (and of the Synoptic and Pauline teaching too); these relate to the function of the Messiah, the salvation of sinners, the ministry of healing, and the gospel of love.

The Qumran ritual washings were no doubt instituted in the light of God's promise in Ezek. 36: 25, that He would purify His people from their uncleanness by sprinkling clean water on them. The same promise also underlies the words of Jesus to Nicodemus

[1]See also Lucetta Mowry, "The Dead Sea Scrolls and the Gospel of John," *The Biblical Archaeologist* 17 (1954), pp. 78 ff.; L. Morris, *The Dead Sea Scrolls and St. John's Gospel* (1960). We should bear in mind, however, that nearly every new discovery in the religious history of the ancient Near East has been hailed as providing the solution to "the problem of the Fourth Gospel"!

in John 3: 5 about the necessity of a new birth "of water and the Spirit" for anyone who would enter the kingdom of God. But in the latter place this new birth is bound up with faith in Jesus and consequent union with Him and sharing of His eternal life. Jesus has filled the old words with a new content.

Such features of early Christian life as baptism and the breaking of bread, the rules of fellowship laid down in Matt. 18, the question of precedence at the Last Supper, the community of goods in the primitive Jerusalem church, the government of the group by apostles, elders and financial officers, have their analogues in the Qumran organization. But their significance within the Christian community is controlled by the person and work of Jesus. This Messiah was different from any kind of Messiah expected at Qumran or elsewhere in Israel in those days, and all the accompaniments of messianic expectation had their meaning transformed in the light of His messianic achievement.

The Qumran covenanters bound themselves by a new covenant, but it was not so new as they thought; it was a specially solemn and binding reaffirmation of the old covenant of Moses' day, by which the people of Israel pledged themselves to obey the law of God. What the people as a whole had failed to do, they themselves would do as a righteous Israel within Israel, and do it so faithfully that their obedience would compensate for their brethren's disobedience. But the new age to which they looked forward was a revival of the best ideals of the old age. They looked forward to a new temple, a pure sacrificial worship, and the reinstatement of a worthy priesthood; but the temple would still be a building made with hands, the sacrificial worship would still involve the slaughter of bulls and goats, the priesthood would still be confined to the sons of Aaron. There is nothing here which presents an affinity to the Johannine narrative of Christ's changing of the water of Jewish purification into the wine of the new age. At Qumran the cadres of priests and Levites were carefully preserved in view of the day when they would resume their service in Jerusalem; there is nothing like this in primitive Christianity. In the early days of the Jerusalem church, we are told, "a great many of the priests were obedient to the faith" (Acts 6: 7); but there is no hint that they retained their priestly status and privileges within the Christian community. On the contrary, the Christian community was taught to consider itself corporately as "a holy priesthood, to offer spiritual sacrifices acceptable to God through Jesus Christ" (1 Pet. 2: 5).

The early Christians, like the men of Qumran, regarded themselves as the Israel of God, the righteous remnant, the little flock, the people of the new covenant. They took over titles given in the

Old Testament to Israel as a whole: they are "a chosen race, a royal priesthood, a holy nation, God's own people" (1 Peter 2: 9). They too believed themselves to be living in the days of the fulfilment of all that the prophets had foretold. Peter's words, "This is that which was spoken by the prophet" (Acts 2: 16), would not surprise us if we met them in a Qumran context. Nor is there any doubt to whom Peter and his associates were indebted for this belief: the Gospels make it plain that this was what their Master taught. Jesus began His ministry in Galilee with the proclamation that the appointed time had fully come and the kingdom of God had drawn near (Mark 1: 15)—words in which it is not difficult to detect an echo of the book of Daniel. We should bear in mind, however, that in His employment of apocalyptic categories as in everything else, Jesus touches nothing that He does not transform. Again, Luke tells us that when Jesus read the opening words of Isaiah 61 in the synagogue at Nazareth, as far as the announcement of "the acceptable year of the Lord," he began His exposition of the text by saying: "Today this scripture has been fulfilled in your hearing" (Luke 4: 16–21). There can, I think, be little question that the main lines of Old Testament interpretation running throughout the New Testament were laid down by Jesus Himself.

The Qumran community believed that the prophets, by divine inspiration and command, foretold the things that were to happen at the end-time, but that one thing was withheld from them—the knowledge of *when* the end-time would come. Without this knowledge it was impossible to understand their oracles properly; they remained a mystery which awaited its true solution. But this knowledge was granted to the Teacher of Righteousness: he was given the key to unlock the divine mysteries, and the special knowledge which God revealed to him was communicated by him to his disciples. No wonder that in their *Hymns of Thanksgiving* they praised God for opening up to them His wonderful mysteries. For *they* understood things which remained a riddle to others. We recall our Lord's words to *His* disciples: "To you has been given the secret of the kingdom of God, but for those outside everything is in parables (or 'riddles')" (Mark 4: 11). The prophets themselves, Peter assures us, did not fully understand the significance of their oracles; "they inquired what person or time was indicated by the Spirit of Christ within them" (1 Pet. 1: 11). But Peter and his fellow-Christians had no need to inquire: they knew the person and they knew the time.

With regard to the interpretation of Old Testament prophecy, then, our Lord did for His followers what the Teacher of Righteousness did for his. But our Lord did more: in the belief of His followers He fulfilled the scriptures in addition to making their meaning plain; He not only disclosed the mystery of the kingdom of God but He came as the very embodiment of that kingdom— the *autobasileia*, as Origen put it. The Qumran interpretation of Old Testament prophecy certainly found references to the Teacher of Righteousness in the prophetic oracles, but did not present him as embodying the fulfilment of those oracles. The fulfilment lay ahead, in the new age, the coming restoration.

In its general biblical interpretation (including its messianic doctrine) the Qumran community laid special stress on the prophetic parts of the Old Testament, in a way which aligns it with Christianity as against rabbinical Judaism. In rabbinical Judaism the prophets tend to be treated by way of commentary on the law; at Qumran, as in the early Church, they were allowed to speak in their own right, and the theology of the two movements is very closely bound up with their respective principles of prophetic interpretation.

The prophetic interpretation adopted by the men of Qumran not only applies the prophetic message to the situation in which they found themselves involved, as the interpretation adopted by the early Christians also did, but "atomizes" the oracles in a way which ignores their original life-setting and general context, and even overrides the plain grammatical connexion between one clause and its neighbour. As Professor Dodd has shown us in *According to the Scriptures* (1952), the New Testament use of the Old Testament exhibits rather an appreciation of the divine pattern of action which pervades the prophetic revelation, and finds that pattern most fully realized in the redemptive act of God in Christ.

Another line of comparison between Qumran and early Christianity has to do with the organization and discipline of the two movements. Here such resemblances as have been noted are of a general rather than an essential character. The Qumran community, like a number of other religious groups, had its purificatory washings, but these lack the distinctive once-for-all element which makes Christian baptism what it is. The Qumran community also had its communal meal, but if we are to suggest a New Testament counterpart for this, we shall find it in the *agape* or love-feast and not in the Lord's Supper; the sacramental and memorial essence of the latter is not paralleled at Qumran. The inspector or superintendent in the Qumran community has little in common with the Christian bishop but the meaning of his title. Even so eschatologically minded a community as the primitive church of Jerusalem did not organize itself in anything like the Qumran manner. The community of goods of which we read in the early chapters of Acts was a spontaneous move rather than a carefully planned and regulated provision, as it was at Qumran. And there is more divergence than resemblance between the fine imposed at Qumran upon any member who deceived the community in the matter of wealth and the fate which befell Ananias and Sapphira when they yielded to the like temptation. Correspondences in detailed points of organization and discipline are less telling than the fact that, whereas the men of Qumran hoped to preserve their holiness by keeping themselves to themselves as far as possible, Jesus consorted with people of all sorts and conditions, and His followers inherited from Him a missionary enthusiasm which, even in its early restriction to "the lost sheep of the house of Israel," has no Qumran counterpart.

There are many parts of the New Testament which have received fresh illumination from the Qumran discoveries; indeed, it would be difficult to think of any part of it which has received no illumination of some sort from them. Even if for the most part they provide us simply with a new background against which we can study the New Testament and the beginnings of Christianity with greater understanding, that is a great contribution. For when any object is viewed against a new background, the object itself takes on a fresh appearance; and against the background supplied by the Qumran discoveries many things in the New Testament take on a new and vivid significance. This is true not only of the Fourth Gospel and other Johannine writings, but of the Synoptic Gospels and the Acts, of the Pauline and other epistles, and not least of the Epistle to the Hebrews.

With regard to the last-named document, it has been argued that the people to whom it was addressed had belonged to the Qumran sect before their conversion to Christianity, and had carried over into Christianity some of their former beliefs and practices, with which the author of the epistle takes issue.[1] This account of the matter can probably not be sustained. But the material which has been adduced in its defence must be added to the evidence already at our disposal for the presence in the early Roman church of elements derived from "sectarian" Judaism. Such elements are attested, for example, by the *Apostolic Tradition* ascribed to Hippolytus, early in the third century.[2] And there is little doubt in my mind that the Epistle to the Hebrews was written to a Jewish-Christian group in Rome in the sixties of the first century.[3] The new evidence, for what it is worth, confirms

[1] *Cf.* Y. Yadin, "The Dead Sea Scrolls and the Epistle to the Hebrews", *Scripta Hierosolymitana* 4 (1957), pp. 36 ff.; also the much more comprehensive work by H. Kosmala, *Hebräer-Essener-Christen* (1959).

[2] *Cf. The Spreading Flame*, pp. 196 f., 253 f.

[3] *Cf. The Spreading Flame*, pp. 152 ff.

the impression already formed by a comparison of certain allusions in this epistle—e.g. the "instruction about ablutions" in Heb. 6: 2—with indications that the Jewish substratum of early Roman Christianity had affinities with some of the "baptist" movements of Palestinian Judaism.

But there is more to be said than this. For the Qumran discoveries have stimulated renewed study of the extent and nature of "sectarian" Judaism in the period immediately preceding and immediately following the birth of Christ. By "sectarian" Judaism is meant a form or forms of Jewish belief and practice deviating from those of the dominant parties, the Pharisees and Sadducees. There is reason to believe that such sectarian Judaism was more widespread than has been generally suspected—not only in Palestine and Transjordan but even farther afield. We have already seen that in addition to the Essenes who lived in separate communities in the wilderness there were adherents of the Essene movement who continued to live in the towns and villages of Palestine, and the same situation probably obtained with regard to the Qumran movement.

Now the particular Jewish environment in which Christianity first began probably partook of this "sectarian" character. In the nativity narrative with which St. Luke's Gospel opens we are introduced to a number of humble and godly Jews—Zechariah and Elizabeth, Joseph and Mary, Simeon and Anna—who were assiduous in their observance of the divine commandments and eagerly awaited "the consolation of Israel." Their piety and hope link them rather with "sectarian" Judaism than with the main stream of national religion. This was the environment into which both John the Baptist and our Lord were born. To this general environment, too, the Essene and Qumran movements belong; to it also, as regards the period with which we are dealing, we must attach the Samaritan community in many of its features. It may not be accidental that on one occasion the Jews of Jerusalem, as they listened to our Lord's teaching, called Him a Samaritan (John 8: 48). He was, of course, no Samaritan; but they recognized something in His teaching that sounded to them much more like the doctrine of the Samaritans than that of their own religious leaders.

But while the resemblances between Christianity and Qumran can be accounted for largely in terms of this common environment, we must not forget those differences between the two which outweigh the resemblances. Christianity cannot be understood simply in terms of its environment—neither, for that matter, can the Qumran movement. The Qumran movement cannot be adequately accounted for apart from the Teacher of Righteousness, and Christianity cannot be adequately accounted for apart from Christ.

The men of Qumran, like the pious community into which Jesus was born, looked for "the consolation of Israel," and expected its consolation to be brought about by the Messiah of David's line. This Messiah, in Qumran expectation, would arise in the last days to deliver Israel, born from the travail of the righteous community. He would be the victorious captain of the sons of light in the last conflict with the sons of darkness, and in the new age following that victory he would enjoy a position as prince, second only to the anointed priest.

In its essentials this expectation of a militant Davidic Messiah was shared by many other Israelites (probably by the vast majority). And Jesus repudiated this kind of Messiahship as wholeheartedly as He could, from the days of the wilderness temptation right on to His death. He did not deny that He was the Messiah of David's line, but He made no such claim publicly, and forbade His disciples to make it on His behalf, because He knew that it would be misunderstood. Indeed, His refusal to accept the kingship which the people of Galilee tried to force upon Him caused considerable disillusionment among many who had followed Him up to that point. If He had envisaged His messianic task as the launching of a holy war, He would have found thousands of enthusiastic and devoted followers. But it is as certain as anything can be that He rejected the whole conception of such a warfare—whether in the Zealot form or in the Qumran form—in favour of the way of the Suffering Servant.

The Qumran covenanters set themselves to fulfil the rôle of the Servant, but they do not appear to have thought of any of their messianic figures as fulfilling it. Jesus, on the other hand, took the fulfilment of the Servant's rôle upon Himself as the very essence of His messianic mission. He combines in His one person the functions of Prophet, Priest and King; Servant of the Lord, Son of Man, and Teacher of Righteousness. In Him the hope of Israel greets its consummation, but in a way which exceeds all expectation. "To him," said one of His disciples (and all the others would have agreed), "all the prophets bear witness that every one who believes in him receives forgiveness of sins through his name" (Acts 10: 43). And if it is true that, after they were forced to abandon their community headquarters, some of the Qumran covenanters made common cause with the refugees from the Jerusalem church, they may have realized that the hopes which their community had cherished so long were fulfilled not in the way which they had expected but by the death and resurrection of Jesus of Nazareth.

Noble as the mission of the Qumran community was, to fill the rôle of the Servant of the Lord, that rôle could never be adequately filled by withdrawal from contact with sinners. The perfect Servant, when He came, was criticized because He welcomed sinners and accepted invitations to their homes. But the Pharisees, who criticized Him thus, would themselves have been criticized by the men of Qumran for their quite inadequate separation from sinners. Yet, if sinners are to be delivered from their sin and changed into new men and women, it must be by one whose friendship towards them is real, unaffected, and unlimited. He who was called the friend of sinners in His lifetime has been known as the friend of sinners ever since.

Ernest Renan described Christianity as "an Essenism which has largely succeeded."[1] Why did it succeed when Essenism disappeared? Partly, I should say, because it contained everything that there was of abiding value in Essenism—and much besides. But, pre-eminently, Christianity owes not only its survival but its very being and character to Jesus. The community of Qumran owed much to the enigmatic figure of the Teacher of Righteousness and his original and inspiring interpretation of prophecy. But Jesus not only interpreted Old Testament prophecy; He carried His interpretation into effect and so became Himself the living fulfilment of Old Testament prophecy. Nor does this fulfilment come to a full stop with His death and resurrection: it goes on in His abiding ministry through His followers, so long as they carry out in His Spirit the charge laid upon the Servant long ago (Isa. 49:6):

> I will give you as a light to the nations,
> That my salvation may reach to the end of the earth.

[1] *Histoire du peuple d'Israel*, v (1893), p. 70.

EPILOGUE

THE story of the Scrolls continues to unfold itself. As soon as public interest appears to be falling off, or discoveries in other places (like the discovery of a Gnostic library near Nag Hammadi in Egypt) promise to steal the limelight from the Dead Sea and its neighbourhood, some new discovery or fresh interpretation brings the Scrolls into the foreground once more.

While the work of publishing the Qumran material is being pushed ahead energetically, discreet but determined endeavours are being made to gain possession of manuscripts (especially some from Cave 11) known to be still in the hands of Bedouin or other unauthorized persons.

*   *   *   *   *

So far as the interpretation of the texts is concerned, one of the most fascinating studies being pursued at present centres around *The Testaments of the Twelve Patriarchs*, described on page 88 as "a pre-Christian Jewish treatise which has come down to us in a Christian recension." This assessment of the treatise is disputed from two sides. On the one hand a Dutch scholar, Dr. M. de Jonge, maintained in a thesis published in 1953 that the treatise is of Christian origin,[1] and finds his views confirmed by the Qumran discoveries, for the Aramaic and Hebrew fragments of the *Testament of Levi* and *Testament of Naphtali* found in the caves present a different text from the corresponding sections of the *Testaments of the Twelve Patriarchs*. They may represent Jewish *sources* of the Christian work. On the other hand, Dr. Marc Philonenko, a French scholar and disciple of Professor Dupont-Sommer, has argued that the complete *Testaments* should now be recognized as a Jewish work, and that passages which were formerly considered to be Christian interpolations in a Jewish work should be accepted as references to Qumran thought and life.[2] He holds that even such certainly Christian passages (as they appear to most readers) as a reference to the crucifixion of the Son of God (*Testament of Levi* 4: 4) are to be interpreted of a Qumran personage—more specifically, the Teacher of Righteous-

---

[1] M. de Jonge, *The Testaments of the Twelve Patriarchs* (1953).

[2] M. Philonenko, *Les interpolations chrétiennes des Testaments des Douze Patriarches et les Manuscrits de Qumrân* (1960).

ness. His arguments have evoked a rejoinder from Dr. de Jonge,[3] and they are in any case open to serious criticism; but the continuing debate is bound to have repercussions on the study of Christian beginnings.[4]

* * * * *

The discoveries in Israel described on page 35 have now been more fully examined. An interesting account of them was given by Dr. Meir Wallenstein of Manchester University in *The Guardian* for February 3 and 4, 1961. The papyrus package found in the goatskin proved to be of special interest. When it was opened by Professor Biberkraut it was found to contain fifteen letters, of which one was written on wood and the rest on papyri. The letter on wood is in Aramaic and begins with the words: "Simeon Bar-Koseba, Prince of Israel, to Jonathan and Masabalah." Like Yeshua Ben-Galgolah in the Murabba'at letters (pp. 32 f.), Jonathan and Masabalah were evidently lieutenants of the guerrilla-leader, commanders of an insurgent garrison in the En-gedi district. Simeon addresses them in the same peremptory and threatening tones as he uses to Yeshua: "Should you not carry out my orders, severe treatment will be meted out to you!"

Of the fourteen letters on papyri, nine are in Aramaic, three in Hebrew, and two in Greek. Most of them are addressed to Jonathan and Masabalah by Simeon himself or members of his staff, and they illustrate the linguistic situation in Judæa at that time.

Dr. Wallenstein thinks that this correspondence must belong to the closing stage of the war of A.D. 132–135, when conditions for the insurgents were becoming increasingly difficult. This appears from one letter which orders the reaping of whatever grain is ripe before the normal time of harvest and the sending of it to Simeon's camp. But even if conditions were difficult, the insurgents did not forget their religious duties; another letter gives directions for making due preparation for the Feast of Tabernacles.

A further expedition by Israeli archaeologists in March 1961 in the same area resulted in fresh discoveries. In the Wadi Heber, where the first discoveries had been made a year earlier, a complete parchment scroll, a papyrus scroll, and scores of folded and crumpled papyri were found; while in the Wadi Mishmar, four miles away, there came to light a cache of 439 objects of copper,

[3] M. de Jonge, "Christian Influence in the Testaments of the Twelve Patriarchs", *Novum Testamentum* 4 (1960), pp. 182 ff.

[4] See also F. M. Braun, "Les Testaments des Douze Patriarches et le Problème de leur Origine", *Revue Biblique* 67 (1960), pp. 516 ff.

bronze and ivory, including implements of war and ritual equipment, from the fourth millennium B.C. The first ten of these latest papyri from the Wadi Heber to be opened proved to be dated legal documents from the period of the war of A.D. 132–135. Other discoveries made in the region indicate that it had undergone at least two earlier phases of human settlement—in the Chalcolithic Age (fourth millennium B.C.) and in the early Israelite period. But, quite apart from the wealth of documentary material from the years of the Bar-Kokhba revolt, the occupation of the caves at this time by the last survivors of the revolt far exceeds the earlier settlements in human interest; for the insurgent units were evidently blockaded there by the Romans until they died of thirst.

It now seems very probable that the "unidentified caves" from which Jordanian Bedouin acquired a haul of manuscript material in 1952 (page 34) were in fact caves in the Wadi Heber.

*   *   *   *   *

The importance of sectarian or nonconformist Judaism as the common environment in which the Qumran community and the primitive Church both originated (page 151) is the main subject of a valuable new study by Principal Matthew Black, entitled *The Scrolls and Christian Origins* (1961).

Still more recently (1964) further excavations at Masada have brought to light many things of interest from the period between its fortification by Herod the Great and its capture by the Romans (see p. 53). The documentary finds at Masada include a Psalter, part of the Hebrew text of Ecclesiasticus (see p. 59), and a liturgical text (the *Rule of Songs for the Sabbath Burnt-Offering*), previously known only from Cave 4 at Qumran.

*   *   *   *   *

No matter at what point one brings the record of the Dead Sea discoveries to a provisional conclusion, it will be very many years before the word "Finis" can be written after the record. Perhaps indeed all that is contained in the foregoing pages is only the beginning.